GW00542694

kick off

OFFICIAL SUPPORTERS GUIDE

THE F.A. PREMIER LEAGUE

THE F.A. PREMIER LEAGUE

LETTER FROM THE CHIEF EXECUTIVE
OF THE PREMIER LEAGUE

After the success and excitement of Euro 96, it is time to focus once more on the domestic season with the Premier League entering its fifth season in very good health.

Many international players, having sampled the unique atmosphere of the English game during Euro 96, will be returning to play in the Premier League, and they, along with our own stars, should ensure that the Premiership enhances further its worldwide reputation for positive and entertaining football.

In England there are large numbers of supporters who regularly attend games, following their teams both home and away, and KICK OFF will enable all these fans, as well as the occasional supporter, to get the most out of the games they attend.

I hope every fan has an enjoyable and entertaining season.

RICK PARRY

Editor . . . . Mike Ivey

Art Director . . . . Atam Sandhu

Designers . . . . Paul Sutcliffe
Steven Clifford

Maps . . . . Ian Bull

Editorial Assistant . . . . . Andrew Templer

Publisher . . . . Simon Rosen

Repro . . . . Colour Origination

Printing . . . . KNP

Special thanks to:
European Stadia - 0151 260 4444

SIDAN ✸ PRESS
PREMIER SPORTS PUBLICATIONS
4 Denbigh Mews, Denbigh Street,
London SW1V 2HQ
Tel: 0171 630 6446 Fax: 0171 233 8905

CONTENTS

ClubCall

The Technology Park, London. NW9 6BS

The F.A. Premier League

16 Lancaster Gate

London W2 3LW

Chairman: **Sir John Quinton**

Chief Executive: **Rick Parry**

Secretary: **Mike Foster**

Assistant Secretary: **Adrian Cook**

Sales & Operations Manager: **Richard Carpenter**

Director of Youth: **Dave Richardson**

CHAMPIONS

1992-1993 **Manchester United**

1993-1994 **Manchester United**

1994-1995 **Blackburn Rovers**

1995-1996 **Manchester United**

F.A. CARLING PREMIERSHIP

HOME TEAM	Arsenal	Aston Villa	Blackburn	Chelsea	Coventry	Derby	Everton	Leeds	Leicester	Liverpool	Man Utd	Middlesboro	Newcastle	Notts Forest	Sheff Wed	Southampton	Sunderland	Tottenham	West Ham	Wimbledon
Arsenal		28/12	19/4	4/9	19/10	7/12	18/1	26/10	12/4	22/3	4/3	1/1	3/5	8/3	16/9	14/12	28/9	24/11	17/8	22/2
Aston Villa	7/9		21/8	26/12	15/2	24/8	5/4	19/10	16/11	1/3	21/9	30/11	11/1	2/11	29/3	11/5	1/2	19/4	15/3	22/12
Blackburn	12/10	22/3		16/11	11/1	9/9	21/9	4/9	11/5	3/11	12/4	21/12	26/12	15/2	22/4	30/11	1/3	17/8	1/2	15/3
Chelsea	5/4	15/9	5/3		24/8	18/1	7/12	3/5	19/4	1/1	22/2	21/8	23/11	28/9	28/12	29/3	15/3	26/10	21/12	19/10
Coventry	23/4	23/11	28/9	12/4		3/5	22/2	14/9	8/3	4/9	18/1	28/12	14/12	17/8	26/10	13/10	1/1	7/12	22/3	5/3
Derby	11/5	12/4	28/12	1/3	30/11		14/12	17/8	2/11	1/2	4/9	17/11	12/10	23/4	1/1	8/3	14/9	22/3	15/2	28/9
Everton	1/3	4/9	1/1	11/5	4/11	15/3		21/12	15/2	23/4	22/3	14/9	17/8	1/2	28/9	16/11	30/11	12/4	12/10	28/12
Leeds	1/2	22/4	5/4	1/12	26/12	29/3	8/3		11/1	16/11	7/9	11/5	21/9	12/10	20/8	15/2	2/11	14/12	1/3	26/8
Leicester	24/8	5/3	7/12	12/10	21/12	22/2	23/11	28/9		15/9	3/5	15/3	26/10	28/12	5/4	21/8	29/3	1/1	23/4	18/1
Liverpool	19/8	18/1	22/2	21/9	5/4	27/10	20/10	5/3	26/12		19/4	29/3	8/3	14/12	7/12	7/9	24/8	3/5	11/1	23/11
Man Utd	16/11	1/1	25/8	2/11	1/3	5/4	21/8	28/12	30/11	12/10		15/2	23/4	14/9	15/3	1/2	21/12	29/9	11/5	29/3
Middlesboro	21/9	3/5	8/3	22/3	7/9	5/3	26/12	7/12	14/12	17/8	23/11		22/2	12/4	18/1	11/1	19/4	19/10	4/9	26/10
Newcastle	30/11	30/9	14/9	15/2	15/3	19/4	29/3	1/1	1/2	23/12	20/10	3/11		11/5	24/8	1/3	5/4	28/12	16/11	21/8
Notts Forest	21/12	22/2	23/11	11/1	29/3	19/10	28/10	19/4	7/9	15/3	26/12	24/8	9/12		5/3	5/4	21/8	18/1	21/9	3/5
Sheff Wed	26/12	17/8	19/10	7/9	1/2	21/9	11/1	22/3	2/9	11/5	14/12	1/3	12/4	18/11		2/11	15/2	8/3	30/11	19/4
Southampton	15/3	7/12	3/5	18/8	19/4	21/12	5/3	23/11	22/3	28/12	26/10	28/9	18/1	4/9	22/2		19/10	14/9	12/4	1/1
Sunderland	11/1	26/10	18/11	15/12	21/9	26/10	3/5	22/2	17/8	12/4	8/3	14/10	4/9	22/3	23/11	22/4		4/3	8/9	7/12
Tottenham	15/2	12/10	29/3	1/2	11/5	21/8	24/8	15/3	22/9	2/12	11/1	23/4	7/9	1/3	21/12	26/12	16/11		2/11	5/4
West Ham	29/3	14/12	26/10	8/3	21/8	23/11	19/4	18/11	19/10	29/9	8/12	5/4	5/3	1/1	3/5	24/8	28/12	22/2		14/9
Wimbledon	2/11	8/3	14/12	22/4	16/11	11/1	7/9	12/4	1/3	15/2	17/8	1/2	22/3	30/11	12/10	23/9	11/5	4/9	26/12	

7

HOLDERS

HOLDERS

Arsenal FC
Arsenal Stadium
Avenell Road, Highbury
London N5 1BU

Club Number: 0171·704·4000
Fax Number: 0171·704·4001
Tickets: 0171·704·4040
Dial A Ticket: 0171·413 3366

INFORMATION HOTLINES

ClubCall: 0891·20 20 20*
Prize Line: 0891·20 20 21*

*Calls cost 49p per minute peak, 39p per minute off peak

CLUB SHOPS

THE GUNNERS SHOP
Located by East Stand
Opening Times:
Monday-Friday 9.30am-5pm
Match Saturdays: 9.30am-Kick Off, plus 30 mins at end
Match Sundays: 10.30am-Kick Off, plus 30 mins at end
Match Evenings: 9.30am-Kick Off, plus 30 mins at end
Tel: 0171·704·4120
Mail Order Service: 0171·354·8397

ARSENAL WORLD OF SPORT
Finsbury Park Station
Opening Times:
Monday-Saturday 9.30am-6pm
Match Sundays: 10.30am-Kick Off, plus 30 mins at end
Match Evenings: 9.30am-Kick Off, plus 30 mins at end
Tel: 0171·272·1000

BOOKING INFORMATION

General Enquiries: 0171·704·4040
Credit Card Bookings: 0171·413·3366
Travel Club: 0171·704·4150
Recorded Info: 0171·704·4242
Junior Gunners: 0171·704·4160

SPECIAL PACKAGES

RESTAURANT FACILITIES
0171·704·4270

CORPORATE HOSPITALITY & SPONSORSHIP
Match Day Packages: £130+VAT
Private Lounges: £2,000+VAT
Sponsorship Packages from £500+VAT
Philip Carling or Yvette Brown 0171·704·4100

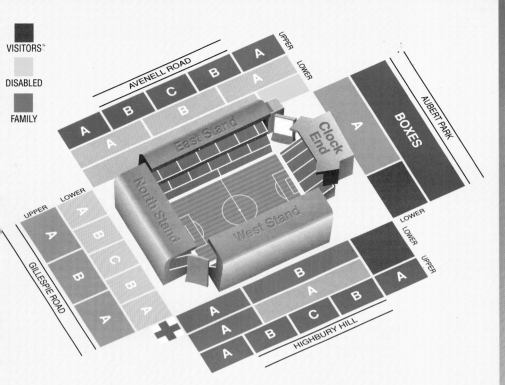

MATCH DAY PRICES

NORTH STAND
Capacity 12,400

UPPER
Block A	£17
Block B	£22

LOWER
Block A	£12
Block B	£13.50
Block C	£17

EAST STAND
Capacity 9,100

UPPER
Block A	£18.50
Block B	£21
Block C	£28

LOWER
Block A	£13.50
Block B	£14.50

WEST STAND
Capacity 11,000

UPPER
Block A	£18.50
Block B	£21
Block C	£28

LOWER
Block A	£14.50

FAMILY
Block A	£13.50
Block B	£14.50
Concessions	£8.00
Jnr Gunners	£7.00

CLOCK END
Capacity 5,900

SINGLE TIER
Block A	£13

FOOD AND DRINK

Bar
Beer	Can	1.65
	1 Pint	2.00
Tea/Coffee/Bovril		0.60
Soft Drinks		0.90-1.00

Food
Quarter Pounder with Cheese	2.00
Burger Deluxe	2.50
Chicken Burger	2.00
Veggie Burger	2.00
Pies	1.60
Jumbo Hot Dog	1.70
Chips	0.75
Sandwiches	2.00-2.50

MISCELLANEOUS INFORMATION

Live music in the North Bank

Jumbotron screens showing highlights and action replays

Gunners Museum open 3 hours before kick off

PROGRAMME: £1.80

GETTING THERE

Arsenal is situated in North London. Parking near the ground is difficult during a match as restrictions come into force. Travel by tube.

DIRECTIONS

From The North:
From the M1 exit at the A1 turn-off - Junction 2/3. The A1 merges for a stretch with the A406. Keep to the A1, soon called Archway Road and then Holloway Road. Turn left onto the A503 Seven Sisters Road and after 1 mile right onto the A1201 Blackstock Road which becomes Highbury Park. Turn right into Aubert Park and right again into Avenell Road.

From The North West:
From the M40 at Junction 1 stay on the A40 for 13 miles and on the A40 (M). At Paddington turn onto the A501. When the A501 becomes Pentonville Road turn left onto Baron Street, signposted as the route for the A1. Take the first right Lion Street and turn left onto the A1. At the Highbury and Islington roundabout, turn right onto St Pauls Road and then left onto the A1201 Highbury Grove. Turn left into Aubert Park and right into Avenell Road.

From The West:
Approaching on the M4 turn left onto the A406 Gunnersbury Avenue at Junction 2. At Hanger Lane turn right onto the A40. Then as route for North West.

From The South West:
Stay on the M3 to end and continue on A316 to Hammersmith. Turn right onto A4 for 1¼ miles, left onto the A3220 Warwick Road and then onto the M41. At end turn onto A40(m) and then as route for North West.

From The East:
From the M11 turn off onto the A406 at Junction 4. and then onto the A503. After Tottenham Hale tube station, turn left into Broad Lane and then back onto the A503 Seven Sisters Road. Turn left onto the A1201 Blackstock Road and then as route for North.

Arsenal is the nearest tube.

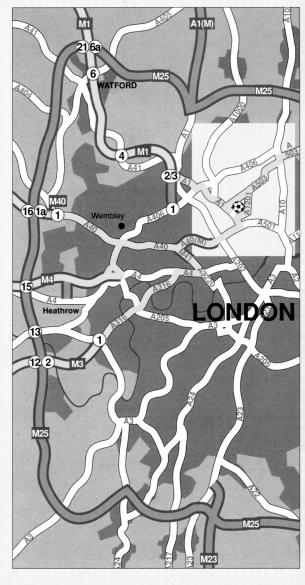

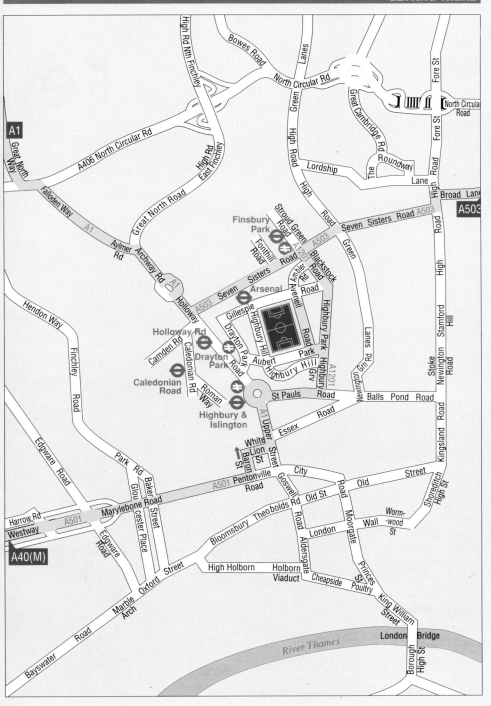

Rely on your **Key** players...

AST
COMPUTER

Aston Villa FC
Villa Park
Trinity Road
Birmingham, B6 6HE

Club Number: 0121·327·2299
Fax Number: 0121·322·2107
Tickets: 0121·327·5353

INFORMATION HOTLINES

ClubCall: **0891·12 11 48***
Recorded Information: 0891·12 18 48*

*Calls cost 49p per minute peak, 39p per minute off peak

CLUB SHOPS

ASTON VILLA SOUVENIR SHOP
Villa Park Stadium
Opening Times:
Monday-Saturday: 9.30am-5pm
Match Saturdays: 9.30am-3.00pm, 5.00pm-6.00pm
Match Sundays: 10.00am-4.00pm, 6.00pm-7.00pm
Match Evenings: 9.30am-7.45pm, 9.45pm-10.00pm
Tel: 0121·327·2800
Fax: 0121·327·7227
Mail Order Service: 0121·327·5963

BOOKING INFORMATION

General Enquiries: 0121·327·5353
Credit Card Bookings: 0121·607·8000
Travel Club: 0121·328·2246

SPECIAL PACKAGES

RESTAURANT FACILITIES
0121·327·5399

STADIUM TOURS
Tammy Williams: 0121·327·2299

CORPORATE HOSPITALITY/SPONSORSHIP/ADVERTISING
Sharon McCullash: 0121·327·5399

CONFERENCE/BANQUETING/EXHIBITIONS/SEMINARS
Range of suites and restaurants accommodating 2-200

WEDDING CEREMONIES AND RECEPTIONS
Catering for all your requirements including
photographer, flowers, cake, cars and entertainment

Contact: Carol Deakin
Catering Sales & Marketing Manager
0121·321·5308

This is my Planet

SMALL LOGO

Reebok

BIG SUPPORTER

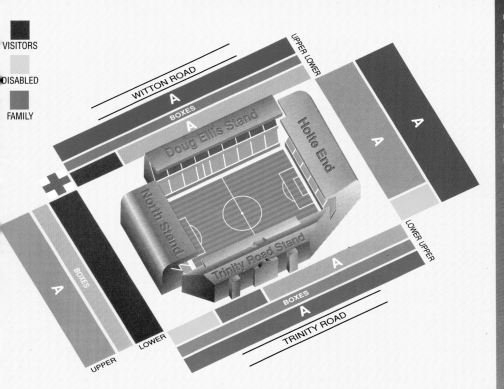

VISITORS

DISABLED

FAMILY

MATCH DAY PRICES

Concession prices in brackets

TRINITY ROAD

Capacity 9,011

UPPER

Block A   £17 (9)

LOWER

Block A   £14 (8)

HOLTE END

Capacity 13,577

UPPER

Block A £15 (7.50)

LOWER

Block A   £13 (6)

NORTH STAND

Capacity 6,876

UPPER

Block A £15 (7.50)

DOUG ELLIS STAND

Capacity 9,639

UPPER

Block A   £17 (9)

LOWER

Block A   £14 (8)

FOOD AND DRINK

Bar

Beer	1 Pint	2.00
Spirits		2.95
Soft Drinks		1.00
Tea/Coffee		0.75

Food

Quarter Pounder	1.90
Cheese Burger	2.00
Jumbo Sausage	1.90
Chips	0.90
Pies/Pasties	1.35
Curry/Rice	2.00
Kingsize Mars/Twix/Snickers	0.60

MISCELLANEOUS INFORMATION

Staged during matches:

5-a-side competitions
Penalty shoot outs
Celebrity presentations

PROGRAMME: £1.50

GETTING THERE

Villa Park is 2 miles north of Birmingham City Centre. Parking is generally available - look for signs.

DIRECTIONS

From The North:
Leave M42 junction 7 onto M6. Exit M6 at junction 6 onto the A38 (M) Aston Expressway. Take first exit right onto Victoria Road. At roundabout take right exit into Witton Road for Villa Park

From The South:
Take M1 to junction 19, then M6. At junction 6 turn onto the A38 (M). Then as route for North.

From The East:
Approaching on the M42, turn off at Junction 8 and get onto the M6 heading towards Birmingham. Then as route for South.

It is a 2 minute walk to the ground from Witton Station.

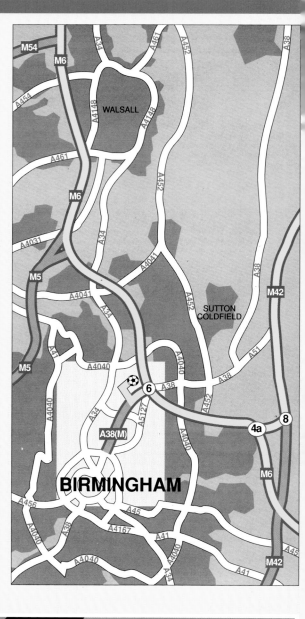

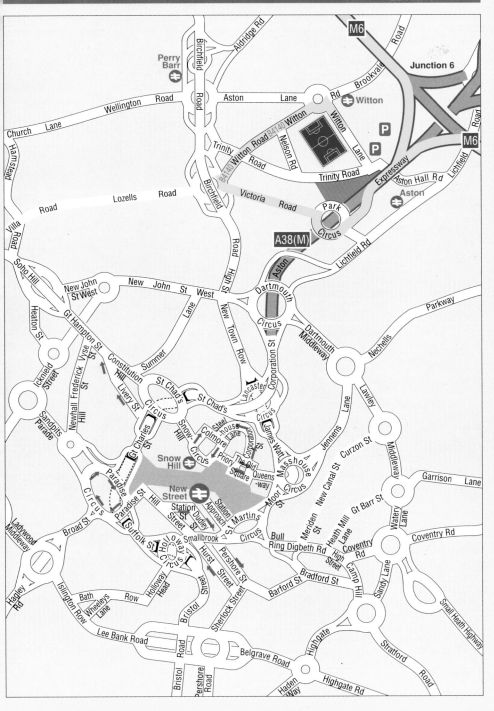

21

WHEREVER YOU GO...

...*we're with you all the way*

RING CIS FREEPHONE

0800 868500

FOR DETAILS OF OUR VALUE FOR MONEY

- *life assurance and savings plans*
- *personal pensions and mortgages*
- *home and motor insurance*

CIS
Co·operative Insurance

SPONSORS OF
BLACKBURN ROVERS

CHIEF OFFICE: MILLER STREET, MANCHESTER M60 0AL.

This leaflet relates to the products of the Co-operative Insurance Society Limited only, which is a member of the CIS marketing group and is regulated by the Personal Investment Authority.

ARTE ET LABORE

Blackburn Rovers FC
Ewood Park
Blackburn
Lancashire BB2 4JF

Club Number: 01254·698888
Fax Number: 01254·671042
Tickets: 01254·671666

INFORMATION HOTLINES

ClubCall: 0891·12 11 79*
Recorded Information: 0891·12 10 14*

*Calls cost 49p per minute peak, 39p per minute off peak

CLUB SHOPS

ROVERSTORE
Ewood Park Stadium
Opening Times:
Monday-Friday: 9.00am-5.30pm
Match Saturdays: 9.30am-3.00pm
Sundays: 11.00am-3.00pm
Non Match Saturday: 9.30am-4.00pm
Tel: 01254·672333
Fax: 01254·673525
Mail Order Service: 01254·672333

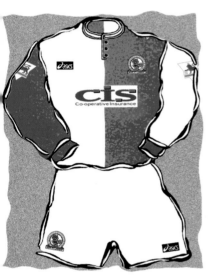

BOOKING INFORMATION

General Enquiries: 01254·671666
Credit Card Bookings: 01254·671666
Travel Club: 01254·698888 Ext 2208

SPECIAL PACKAGES

RESTAURANT FACILITIES
01254·691919

STADIUM TOURS
01254·671888

CORPORATE HOSPITALITY/SPONSORSHIP
01254·690909

MATCH BALL
01254·690909

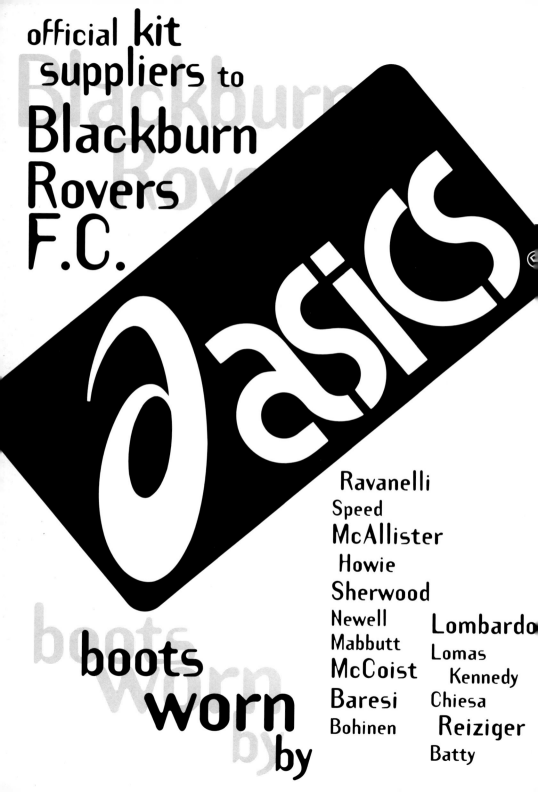

official **kit**
suppliers to
Blackburn
Rovers
F.C.

asics

boots
worn
by

Ravanelli
Speed
McAllister
Howie
Sherwood
Newell
Mabbutt
McCoist
Baresi
Bohinen

Lombardo
Lomas
Kennedy
Chiesa
Reiziger
Batty

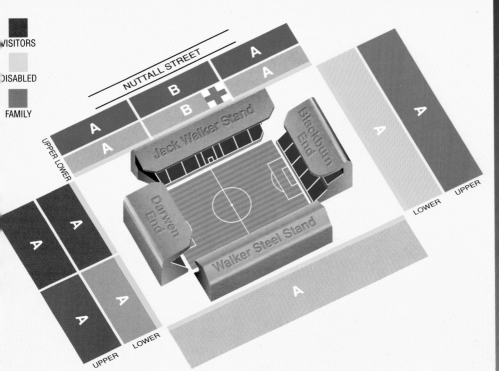

VISITORS

DISABLED

FAMILY

NUTTALL STREET

A

A

B

B

Jack Walker Stand

Blackburn End

UPPER LOWER

A

A

Darwen End

Walker Steel Stand

A

A

A

A

A

A

LOWER UPPER

UPPER LOWER

MATCH DAY PRICES

Concession prices in brackets

JACK WALKER

Capacity 11,000

UPPER	
Block A	£18 (9)
Block B	£19

LOWER	
Block A	£15 (8)
Block B	£18 (9)

WALKER STEEL

Capacity 5,000

LOWER	
Block A	£15 (8)

BLACKBURN END

Capacity 8,000

FAMILY	
Block A	£15 (8)

LOWER	
Block A	£15 (8)

DARWEN END

Capacity 8,000

UPPER	
Block A	£15 (8)

LOWER	
Block A	£15 (8)

FOOD AND DRINK

Bar
Licensed bars in all concourses serving a variety of refreshments

Food
Fast Food snack bars serving a variety of snacks

MISCELLANEOUS INFORMATION

Staged during matches:

Rovers Return Lottery Draw

Double Your Money Prize Draw

PROGRAMME: £1.50

GETTING THERE

Blackburn Rovers are situated a mile from Blackburn town centre in Ewood Park. Car parking can be found at Albion Road and Hollin Bridge Street.

DIRECTIONS

From The North and South:
Exit M6 at junction 31 onto A59/A677 towards Blackburn. After 1½ miles the road splits. Keep to the A677. After approximately 5 miles turn right at the Esso garage onto Montague Street, cross over King Street into Byron Street, left into Canterbury Street and follow the one-way system until the T-junction with the Bolton Road A666. Turn right for Ewood Park.

From The South:
Exit M61 junction 8 onto A674. After 5 miles turn right onto the A6062 for 3 miles until the Bolton Road A666. Turn right and Ewood Park is ¼ mile down on your left.

From The East:
Exit M65 junction 6, turn left onto the A6119 Whitebirk Road for ½ mile, turn right onto the A677 for ½ mile and then bear left onto the A679 for 1 mile, then left onto the A666 for 1¼ miles. Ewood Park is on the left.

Blackburn Station is well served for buses to ground.

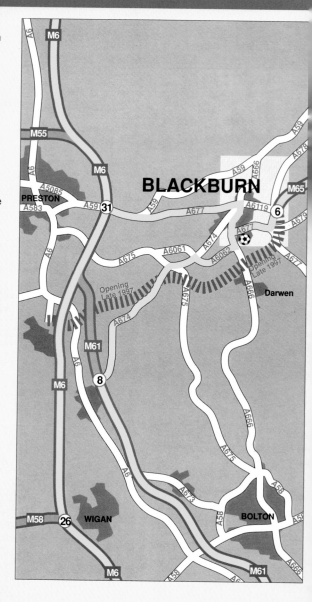

THE LIVE
ACTION STATION

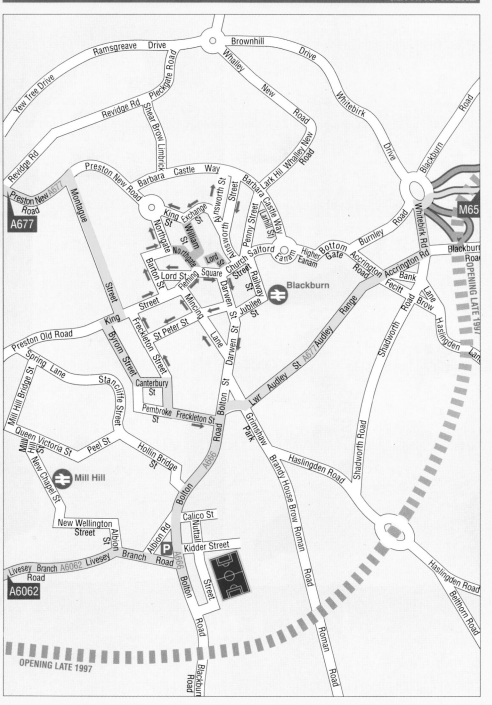

LEGENDS

Peter Osgood is a Chelsea Legend. Few true fans will forget his battles with Leeds United, his crucial diving header in the 1970 FA Cup Final Replay at Old Trafford or that amazing left-footer at Stamford Bridge which the AC Milan goalkeeper probably never saw. It's the same with Coors Extra Gold, the Rocky Mountain Legend. Coors is a full bodied, premium lager with a taste that few true lager fans forget, in cans, bottles and on draught.

Coors is the official sponsor of Chelsea Football Club.

Chelsea FC
Stamford Bridge
Fulham Road
London SW6 1HS

Club Number: **0171·385·5545**
Fax Number: **0171·381·4831**
Tickets: **0171·386·7799**

INFORMATION HOTLINES

ClubCall: **0891·12 11 59***
Recorded Info: **0891·12 10 11***

Calls cost 49p per minute peak, 39p per minute off peak

CLUB SHOPS

CHELSEA SPORTSLAND
394-400 Fulham Road
London SW6 1HW
Opening Times:
Monday-Saturday: 9.00am-5.00pm
Match Saturdays: 9.00am-6.00pm
Match Sundays: 10.30am-6.00pm
Match Evenings: 9am-10pm
Tel: 0171·381·4569
Fax: 0171·381·5697
Mail Order Service: 0171·381·4569

BOOKING INFORMATION

General Enquiries: 0171·385·5545
Credit Card Bookings: 0171·386·7799
Travel Club: 0171·385·5545
Chelsea Worldwide Travel 0171·381·5500
Chelsea Pitchowners 0171·610·2235
Bridge Builder Promotions 0171·386·5557

SPECIAL PACKAGES

RESTAURANT FACILITIES/MATCH BALL
Marketing Department 0171·385·7809

STADIUM TOURS
Fridays 11.00am-1.00pm
Shaun Gore 0171·385 0710

CORPORATE HOSPITALITY/SPONSORSHIP
Carole Phair, Commercial Manager 0171·385·7809

CONFERENCE AND BANQUETING
Debra Ware 0171·385·7980

Life is a game. And we all know which one.

UMBRO®
The heart and soul
of football.™

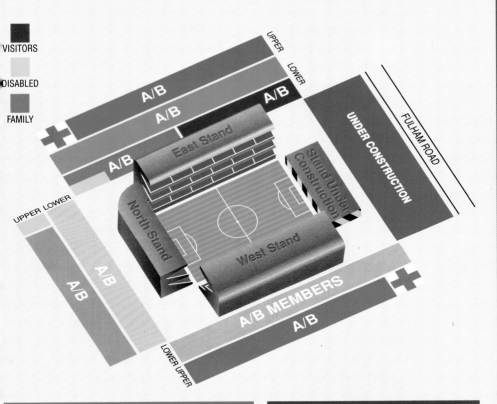

VISITORS

DISABLED

FAMILY

MATCH DAY PRICES

Concession prices in brackets

WEST STAND
Capacity 6,056

UPPER

Category A	£20
Category B	£15

LOWER

Category A	£13 (6)
Category B	£10 (5)

NORTH STAND
Capacity 8,600

UPPER

Category A	£20
Category B	£15

LOWER

Category A	£20
Category B	£15

EAST STAND
Capacity 11,160

UPPER

Category A	£25
Category B	£17

MIDDLE

Category A	£40
Category B	£25

FAMILY

Category A	£20
Category B	£16

VISITORS

Category A	£20
Category B	£18

SOUTH STAND
Under Construction

FOOD AND DRINK

Bar

Beer	1/2 Pint	1.10
	1 Pint	2.20
Spirits		1.60
Soft Drinks		1.00

Food

Quarter Pounder	2.50
Cheese Burger	3.00
Jumbo Hot Dog	2.50
Chips	1.00
Sandwiches	2.00
Confectionery	0.50

MISCELLANEOUS INFORMATION

Senior and Junior player presentations

Latest chart music over the Tannoys

PROGRAMME: £2.00

GETTING THERE

Chelsea play at Stamford Bridge in central London. Parking restrictions during the game make it advisable to park away from the ground and travel by Tube.

DIRECTIONS

From The North:
From the M1 turn off onto the A406 North Circular Road at Junction 1.Turn off onto the A40 and stay on until the junction with the M41. Turn right onto the M41 and continue for 1 mile before turning onto the A3220 Holland Road. Follow the A3220 for 2 miles before turning right onto the A304 Fulham Road. Stamford Bridge is quarter of a mile along on the right.

From The North West:
From the M40, continue into the A40 and stay on until the junction with the M41. Then as route for North.

From The West:
Get on the M4 and at Junction 1 continue along the A4 for 4 miles until it becomes the Cromwell Road. Turn right onto the A3220 Earls Court Road then as route for North.

From The South West:
From the M3 turn off onto the M25 at Junction 2. Continue for 10 miles until you reach Junction 15 at which point turn off onto the M4. Then as route for the West.

The nearest tube station is Fulham Broadway on the District Line.

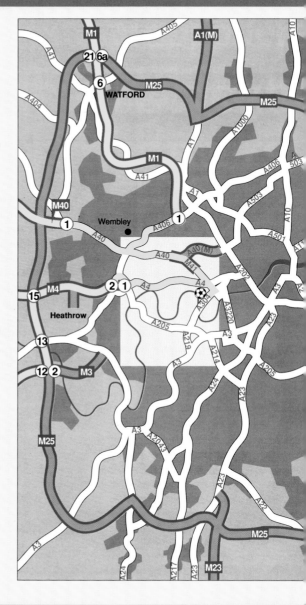

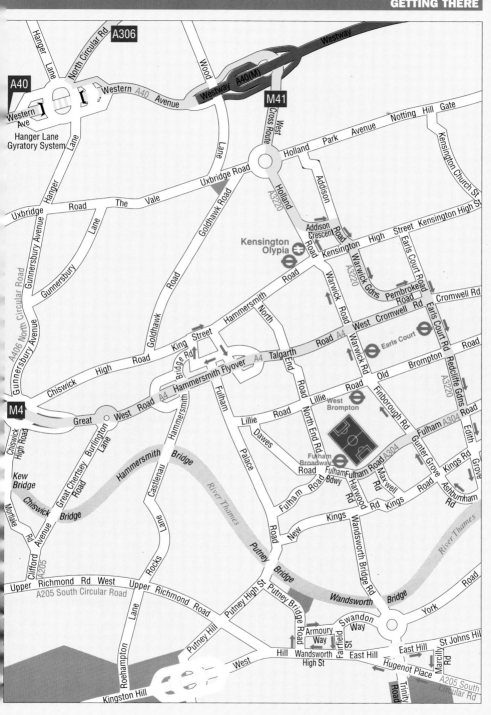

THE NUMBER TO WATCH.

**FOR INFORMATION
ON THE PEUGEOT 406 CALL
0345 000 406**

406
PEUGEOT

THE DRIVE OF YOUR LIFE

Coventry City FC
Highfield Road Stadium
King Richard Street
Coventry CV2 4FW

Club Number: 01203·234010
Fax Number: 01203·234015
Tickets: 01203·234000

INFORMATION HOTLINES

ClubCall: 0891·12 11 66*
*Calls cost 49p per minute peak, 39p per minute off peak

CLUB SHOPS

COVENTRY CITY FC SHOP
Highfield Road Stadium
Opening Times:
Monday-Saturday: 9.00am-6.00pm
Match Saturdays: 9.00am-5.00pm
Match Sundays: 10.30am-5.00pm
Match Evenings: 9am-10pm
Tel: 01203·234000
Fax: 01203·234015

SKY BLUE LEISURE
Cathedral Lanes Shopping Centre, Coventry
Opening Times
Monday-Saturday: 9.00am-5.30pm
Match Saturdays: 9.00am-5.30pm
Match Sundays: 9.00am-5.30pm
Match Evenings: 9am-5.30pm
Tel: 01203·633619

BOOKING INFORMATION

General Enquiries: 01203·234000
Credit Card Bookings: 01203·578000
Travel Club: 01203·633127
Recorded Info: 01203·234000

SPECIAL PACKAGES

RESTAURANT FACILITIES
Lesley 01203·234015

STADIUM TOURS/CORPORATE HOSPITALITY/
SPONSORSHIP/MATCH BALL
Marketing Department, 01203·234010

The World Of Le Coq Sportif

Official kit suppliers
to over 40
professional clubs

Football Authentiqué

lecoqsportif®

OFFICIAL KIT SUPPLIER TO
COVENTRY CITY FOOTBALL CLUB

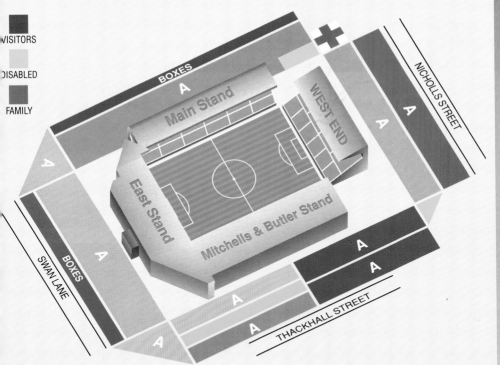

VISITORS

DISABLED

FAMILY

BOXES
A
Main Stand

WEST END

NICHOLLS STREET

A

A

A

East Stand

Mitchells & Butler Stand

A

A

A

A

SWAN LANE

BOXES

A

A

THACKHALL STREET

MATCH DAY PRICES

Concession prices in brackets

M&B STAND

Capacity 6,100

UPPER

Block A   £18 (9)

LOWER

Block A   £18 (9)

VISITORS

Block A   £18 (10)

MAIN STAND

Capacity 3,300

SINGLE TIER

Block A   £20 (10)

WEST END

Capacity 6,000

FAMILY

Block A £15 (7.50)

LOWER

Block A £15 (7.50)

EAST STAND

Capacity 5,100

SINGLE TIER

Block A   £18 (9)

FOOD AND DRINK

Bar

Bitter	TBA
Lager	TBA
Tea/Coffee	TBA
Soft Drinks	TBA

Food

Hamburger	TBA
Pies/Pasties	TBA
Chicken Burger	TBA
Curry and Rice	TBA

MISCELLANEOUS INFORMATION

HOSPITALITY IN CARLING SUITE:

- **3 Course Meal**
- **Tour of Stadium**
- **Seats in Directors Box**

PROGRAMME: £1.50

GETTING THERE

Coventry City play at the Highfield Road Stadium, less than a mile from the city centre. There is some car parking off Kingsway.

DIRECTIONS

From The North:
Take the M1 to Junction 21 and join the M69 continuing at Junction 2 onto the A4600 following signs to the centre. This road becomes the Walsgrave Road which turns right into Swan Lane. The ground is ahead on the left.

From The South:
Approaching on the M40, turn off at Junction 15 onto the A46. Continue on the A46 for approximately 10 miles, then the A444, turning right onto the A4082 London Road and left at the roundabout onto the B4110 Humber Road. Go straight across the crossroads into Swan Lane and the ground is ahead on the left.

From The West/East:
Approaching on the M6 in either direction, turn off onto the A4600 at Junction 2. Then as route for North.

From The East:
Approaching from the East on the M45, exit at Junction 1 onto the A45 which becomes the A423. Go straight ahead at the roundabout into the B4110 London Road which becomes the Humber Road. Then as route for South.

Coventry Railway Station is situated one mile from the ground. Buses leave from Trinity Street Bus Station.

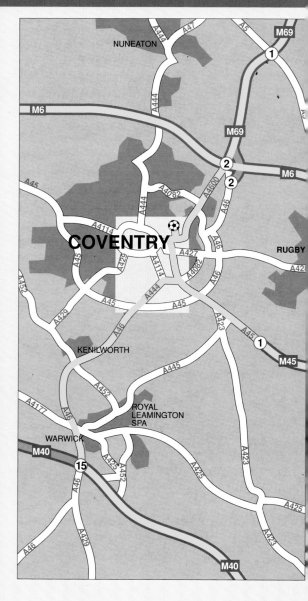

BBC Radio **West Midlands**
95.6FM

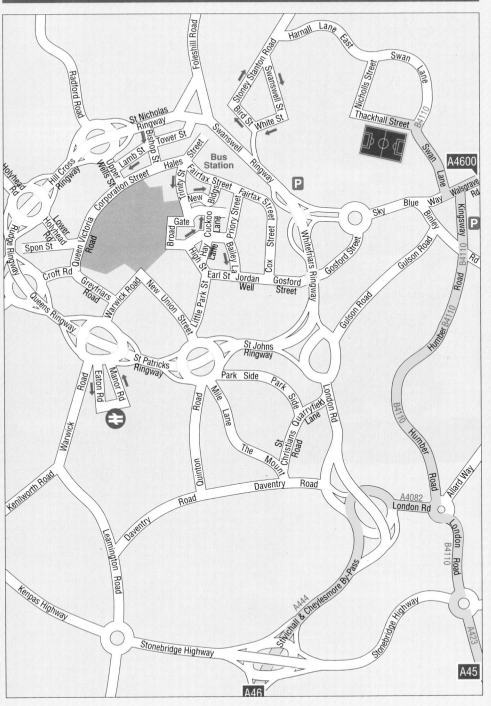

Derby County FC
The Baseball Ground
Shaftesbury Crescent
Derby DE23 8NB

Club Number: 01332·340105
Fax Number: 01332·360988
Tickets: 0891·33 22 13*

INFORMATION HOTLINES

ClubCall: 0891·12 11 87*

*Calls cost 49p per minute peak, 39p per minute off peak

CLUB SHOPS

RAMTIQUE
The Baseball Ground
Opening Times
Monday-Friday 9.00am-5pm
Match Saturdays: 9.00am-Kick Off, plus 30 mins at end
Match Sundays: 9.00am-Kick Off, plus 30 mins at end
Match Evenings: 9.00am-Kick Off, closed after game
Non-Match Saturdays: 9.00am-1.00pm
Tel: 01332·292081
Fax: 01332·360988
Mail Order Service: 01332·292081

BOOKING INFORMATION

General Enquiries: 01332·340105
Credit Card Bookings: 01332·203030
Travel Club: 01332·340105
Recorded Info: 01332·203030

SPECIAL PACKAGES

RESTAURANT FACILITIES
Ted Gascoyne, 01332 340105

STADIUM TOURS
Steve Bradshaw, 01332·340105

**CORPORATE HOSPITALITY/
SPONSORSHIP/MATCH BALL**
Colin Tunnicliffe, 01332 340105

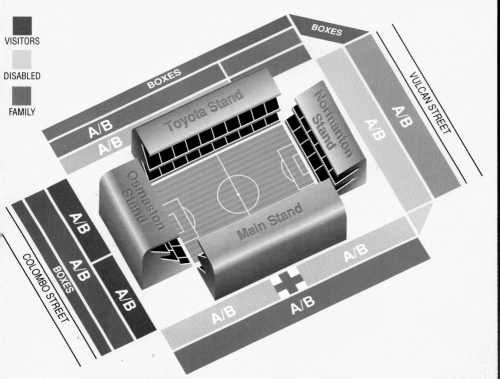

VISITORS

DISABLED

FAMILY

BOXES

BOXES

VULCAN STREET

A/B

A/B

A/B

Toyota Stand

Normanton Stand

Osmaston Stand

Main Stand

A/B

A/B

COLOMBO STREET

BOXES

A/B

A/B

A/B

A/B

A/B

MATCH DAY PRICES

MAIN STAND		**TOYOTA STAND**	
UPPER		**UPPER**	
Block A	£17	Block A	£17
Block B	£18	Block B	£18
LOWER		**LOWER**	
Block A	£17	Block A	£17
Block B	£18	Block B	£18

OSMASTON END		**NORMANTON STAND**	
UPPER		**UPPER**	
Block A	£17	Block A	£17
Block B	£18	Block B	£18
LOWER		**LOWER**	
Block A	£17	Block A	£17
Block B	£18	Block B	£18
VISITORS			
Block A	£17		
Block B	£18		

FOOD AND DRINK

Bar

Beer	Bitter	1.75
	Lager	1.85
Tea		0.50
Coffee		0.70
Soft Drinks		0.70

Food

Pies and pasties	1.30
Quarter Pounder	1.90
Hot Dog	1.90

MISCELLANEOUS INFORMATION

Staged during matches:

Penalty Shoot Outs

Premium Club Prize Draw

PROGRAMME: £1.50

SHRUG OFF WATER AND MIDFIELD TERRIERS

WATER-RESISTANT

PITTARDS LEATHER

PUMA
KING

GETTING THERE

Derby County play at the Baseball Ground, south of the city centre in an area dominated by industrial units. There is some car parking on Osmaston Road

DIRECTIONS

From The North:
Approaching on the M1 take the exit at Junction 25 and get onto the A52. After 5 miles turn left onto the A5111 Raynesway. At the double roundabout turn right onto Harvey Road and at the Spider Bridge roundabout turn right onto the Osmaston Road. Continue for approximately 1½ miles and turn left into Shaftesbury Street. Colombo Street is on the right and the ground straight ahead.

From The South:
Approaching on the M1 take the exit at Junction 24 and get onto the A6. Follow the road for 7 miles until the roundabout with the ring road. Turn left onto the A5111 Harvey Road. and right at Spider Bridge onto Osmaston Road. Then as route for the North.

Derby Railway Station is about one mile from the ground and is a 20 minute walk. Buses run from the city centre to the ground.

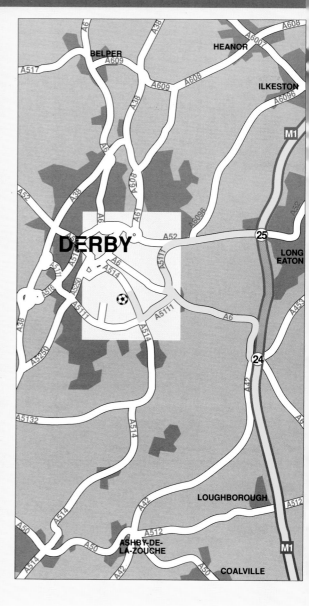

DERBY COUNTY

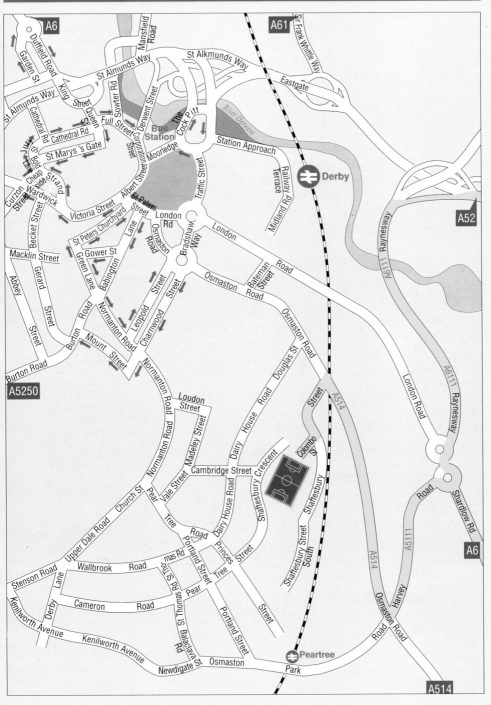

Everton FC
Goodison Park
Goodison Road
Liverpool L4 4EL

Club Number: **0151·330·2200**
Fax Number: **0151·286·9112**
Tickets: **0151·330·2300**

INFORMATION HOTLINES

ClubCall: **0891·12 11 99***
Recorded Information **0891·12 15 99***
*Calls cost 49p per minute peak, 39p per minute off peak

CLUB SHOPS

EVERTON FC MEGASTORE
Walton Lane
Opening Times:
Monday-Friday 9.00am-5.00pm
Match Saturdays: 9.30am-3.00pm, 4.30pm-5.15pm
Match Sundays: 9.00am-3.00pm, 4.30pm-5.15pm
Match Evenings: 9.00am-7.30pm, 9.00pm-9.45pm
Non match Saturdays: 9.00am-5.00pm
Tel: 0151·330·2030
Fax: 0151·286·0100
Mail Order Service: 0151·330·2333

EVERTON FC COLLECTION
Gwladys Street
Goodison Park
Opening Times:
Match Saturdays: 9.30am-3.00pm, 4.30pm-5.15pm
Match Sundays: 9.00am-3.00pm, 4.30pm-5.15pm
Match Evenings: 9.00am-7.30pm, 9.00pm-9.45pm

BOOKING INFORMATION

General Enquiries:	0151·330·2200
Credit Card Bookings:	0151·471·8000
Travel Club:	0151·330·2266
Entertainment Complex:	0151·330·2499
Commercial Club:	0151·330·2224

SPECIAL PACKAGES

RESTAURANT FACILITIES
John Rotheram 0151·330·2499

STADIUM TOURS
0151·330·2266

**CORPORATE HOSPITALITY/
SPONSORSHIP/MATCH BALL**
0151·330·2400

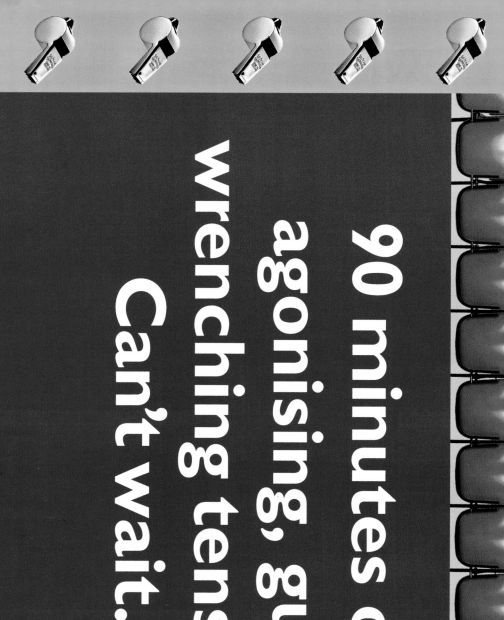

90 minutes of agonising, gut wrenching tension. Can't wait.

UMBRO ®
The heart and soul
of football.™

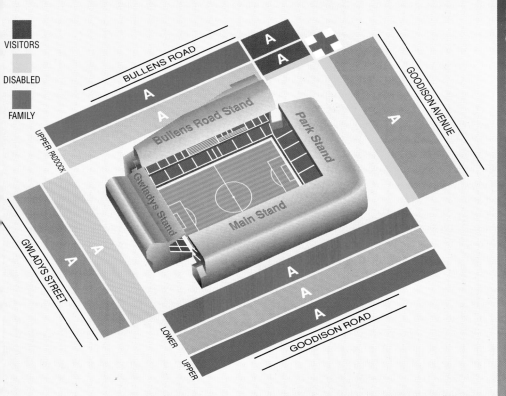

VISITORS

DISABLED

FAMILY

MATCH DAY PRICES

MAIN STAND
Capacity 6,271

UPPER	
Block A	£15
Juniors	£7

MIDDLE	
Block A	£18

FAMILY	
Block A	£15
Juniors	£7
Seniors	£9

GWLADYS STAND
Capacity 7,892

UPPER	
Block A	£15
Seniors	£9

LOWER	
Block A	£13
Juniors	£7

BULLENS ROAD
Capacity 5,726

UPPER	
Block A	£17

VISITORS	
Block A	£17

LOWER	
Block A	£15
Juniors	£7
Seniors	£9

VISITORS	
Block A	£15
Seniors	£10

PARK END STAND
Capacity 5,888

SINGLE TIER	
Block A	£16

FOOD AND DRINK

Bar

Lager	1.70
Bitter	1.70
Yates White Wine	1.60
Tea/Coffee	0.90
Hot Chocolate/Bovril	0.90
Pepsi (500mls)	1.00
Mineral Water (500mls)	1.00

Food

Meat Pie	1.30
Jumbo Sausage Roll	1.10
Hot Dogs	1.70
Pizza	1.70
Breakfast in Bap	2.00
Chocolate Eclairs	0.40
Everton Mints	1.40

MISCELLANEOUS INFORMATION

Radio Everton broadcasts on matchdays on 1602AM

PROGRAMME: £1.70

GETTING THERE

Everton's Goodison Park is situated two miles north of Liverpool City Centre, opposite Stanley Park. Car parking is available in Anfield Road.

DIRECTIONS

From the North:
Approaching on the M6, exit at Junction 26 onto the M58 and continue until the end. At Junction 7 turn left onto the A59 Ormskirk Road. Continue on this road as it becomes Rice Lane, and cross over the roundabout into County Road. After ¼ mile turn left into Everton Valley and then Walton Lane. Goodison Road and the ground are on the left.

From the South:
Approaching on the M6, exit at Junction 21a onto the M62. Exit the M62 at Junction 4 and get onto the A5080. At the junction with the A5058 turn right and continue along this road as it becomes Queens Drive. Continue to the junction with Walton Hall Avenue and turn left onto the A580 Walton Lane. Goodison Road and the ground are on the right.

From the East:
Approaching on the M62 exit at Junction 4 and get onto the A5058. Then as route for the South.

Lime Street Railway Station is in the town centre, 2 miles from Goodison Park. Kirkdale Railway Station is a 10 minute walk from the ground.

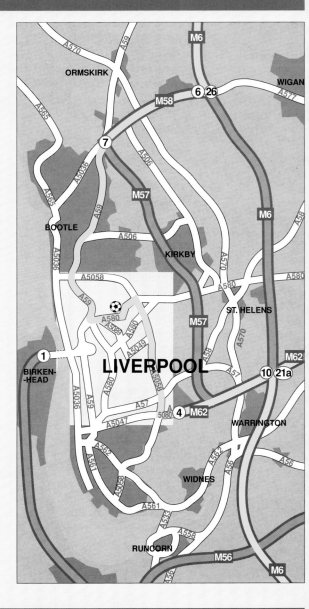

EVERTON RADIO

1602 AM

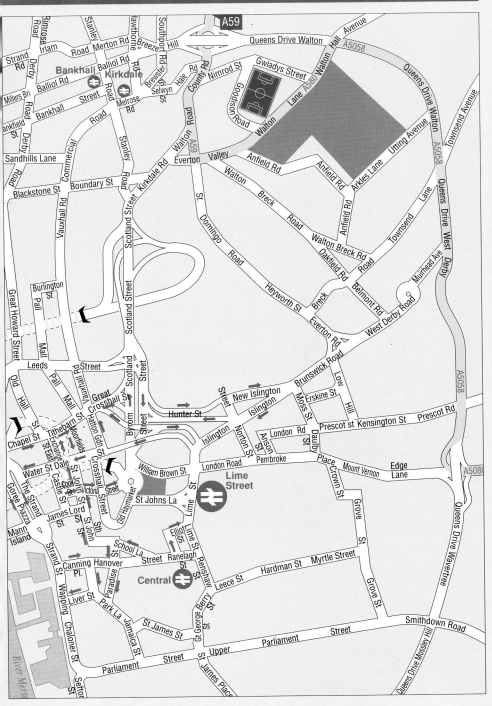

EVERTON

Packard Bell

Work Hard, Play Hard

Worldwide Multimedia PC Leader

Available in Dixons, Currys and PC World
For your nearest Dixons or Currys store call 0181·200·0200
For your nearest PC World store call 0990·464464

Leeds United AFC
Elland Road
Leeds LS11 0ES

Club Number: **0113·271·6037**
Fax Number: **0113·270·6560**
Tickets: **0113·271·0710**

INFORMATION HOTLINES

ClubCall: **0891·12 11 80***
Recorded Information: 0891·12 16 80*

*Calls cost 49p per minute peak, 39p per minute off peak

CLUB SHOPS

LEEDS UNITED COLLECTION
Elland Road
Opening Times:
Monday-Friday 9.00am-5.00pm (9.00am-5.00pm Thursday)
Match Saturdays: 9.00am-6.00pm
Match Sundays: 9.00am-6.00pm
Match Evenings: 9.00am-one hour after game end
Tel: 0113·225·1144
Fax: 0113·226·6083
Mail Order Service: 0113·270·3077

LEEDS UNITED COLLECTION
1: 10/11 Burton's Arcade, Leeds
2: 16 Little Westgate, Wakefield
Opening Times:
Monday-Saturday 9.30am-5.15pm

BOOKING INFORMATION

General Enquiries: 0113·271·0710
Credit Card Bookings: 0113·271·0710
Travel Club: 0113·271·6037
Lottery/Cashline: 0113·277·1170
Football In The Community: 0113·277·9851

SPECIAL PACKAGES

RESTAURANT FACILITIES
Banqueting Department: 0113·272·0492

STADIUM TOURS
Dick Wright: 0113·271·6037

COMMERCIAL HOSPITALITY
0113·271·0168

SPONSORSHIP/MATCH BALL
Match Sponsors Packs from £3250
Ball Sponsors from £500
0113·271·0168

LEEDS UNITED

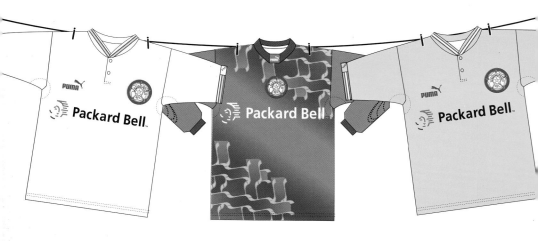

THREE SHIRTS ON A LINE.

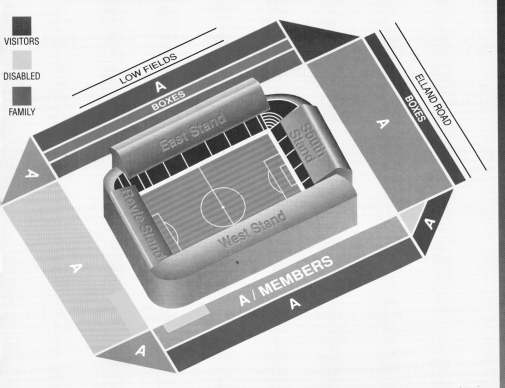

VISITORS

DISABLED

FAMILY

MATCH DAY PRICES

Concession prices in brackets

WEST STAND

UPPER	
Cat A+	£25
Cat A	£22
Cat B	£21
Cat C	£20

LOWER	
Cat A+	£25
Cat A	£22
Cat B	£21
Cat C	£20

REVIE STAND

SINGLE TIER	
Cat A+	£19
Cat A	£16
Cat B	£15
Cat C	£14

NE/NW STANDS	
Cat A+	£21
Cat A	£18
Cat B	£17
Cat C	£16

EAST STAND

UPPER	
Cat A+	£23
Cat A	£20
Cat B	£19
Cat C	£18

FAMILY	
Cat A+	£21
Cat A	£18
Cat B	£17
Cat C	£16

SOUTH STAND

SINGLE TIER	
Cat A+	£19
Cat A	£16
Cat B	£15
Cat C	£14

STAND B	
Cat A+	£19
Cat A	£16
Cat B	£15
Cat C	£14

FOOD AND DRINK

Bar

Beer	Bitter	1.90
	Lager	2.00
Tea/Coffee		0.70
Soft Drinks		0.95
Kia Ora		0.65

Food

Burger	1.90
Jumbo Hot Dog	1.90
Pies/Pasties	1.40
Chips	0.90
Mars/Snickers/Twix	0.60

MISCELLANEOUS INFORMATION

The Club has its own matchday radio station, Radio Leeds United, broadcasting on 1323 A.M. with match news, interviews, travel and parking updates.

PROGRAMME: £1.70

GETTING THERE

Elland Road is situated two miles south-west of the city centre. There are two car parks adjacent to the ground and some parking is to be found in the Heath Grove vicinity.

DIRECTIONS

From The North:
Approaching on the A1, turn off onto the A58 and continue for 13 miles. Take the A58(M) for a further half mile, turning left onto the A643. Continue across the M621, turning right into Elland Road. The ground is on the right.

From The South:
Approaching from the south on the M1, continue on the M621 until Junction 2, turning left onto the A643. Then as route for the North.

From The West/East:
Approaching on the M621, turn onto the A643 at Junction 2. Then as route for North.

Leeds Railway Station is located in the city centre approximately 2 miles away. Buses operate from Sovereign Street to the ground.

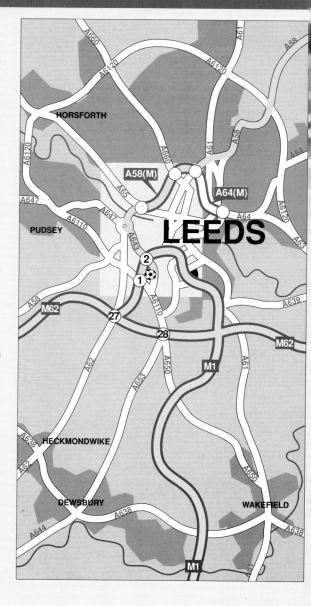

LEEDS UNITED

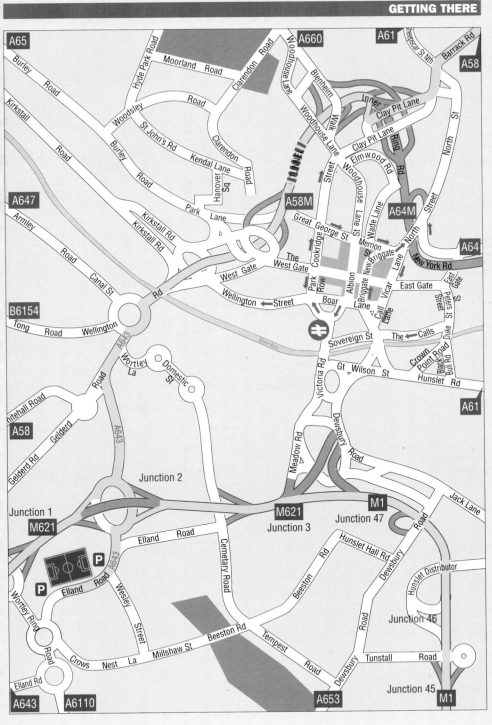

KEEP ON THE BALL!

You never know <u>who</u> is trying to get their hands on your NEW Walkers Barbecue Flavour Crisps

Leicester City FC
Filbert Street
Leicester
LE2 7FL

Club Number: 0116·255·5000
Fax Number: 0116·247·0585
Tickets: 0116·291·5232

INFORMATION HOTLINES

ClubCall: 0891·12 11 85*
Information 0891·12 10 28*

*Calls cost 49p per minute peak, 39p per minute off peak

CLUB SHOPS

SHOP 1
Filbert Street
Opening Times:
Monday-Friday 9.00am-5.30pm
Match Saturdays: 9.00am-3.00pm, 4.45pm-5.15pm
Match Sundays: 9.00am-4.00pm, 5.45pm-6.15pm
Match Evenings: 9.00am-8.00pm
Tel: 0116·291·5253
Fax: 0116·247·0585
Mail Order Service: 0116·291·5226

SHOP 2
28 Churchgate
Opening Times:
Monday-Friday: 9.00am-5.30pm
Match Saturdays: 9.00am-5.30pm
Match Evenings: 9.00am-5.30pm
Tel: 0116·291·5210
Fax: 0116·247·0585
Mail Order Service: 0116·291·5226

BOOKING INFORMATION

General Enquiries: 0116·291·5232
Credit Card Bookings: 0116·291·5232
Travel Club: 0116·255·5000

SPECIAL PACKAGES

RESTAURANT FACILITIES
Fosse Restaurant: 0116·291·5050

STADIUM TOURS
0116·291·5223

CORPORATE HOSPITALITY/SPONSORSHIP/MATCH BALL
0116·291·5251

LOTTERIES
0116·291·5115

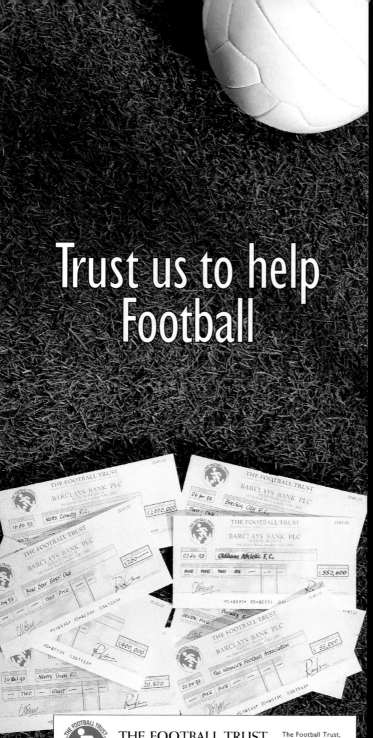

Trust us to help Football

MAJOR PROJECTS

The Trust's main task is to help League clubs to implement the Taylor Report. Since 1990, over £136m has been awarded towards ground improvements costing some £418m. In its 20 years the Trust has received £250 million from Littlewoods, Vernons and Zetters and Littlewoods Spot the Ball..

CCTV

The introduction of CCTV throughout football has been the most important measure in the campaign against hooliganism. CCTV is an initiative pioneered by the Trust. Since 1979 nearly £6m has been awarded towards the installation and upgrading of equipment.

SAFETY AND IMPROVEMENTS

Initiatives to improve the safety and comfort of spectators and to upgrade facilities for families, for supporters with disabilities, for women and for community use are grant aided by the Trust from funds donated by Littlewoods Pools from their Spot the Ball competition.

GRASS ROOTS

The Trust is helping the game at all levels. Part of the Spot the Ball funding is dedicated to assisting clubs outside the full-time leagues. Schemes include safety work, upgrading pitch and changing facilities and providing kit and equipment to junior teams.

THE FOOTBALL TRUST
Helping the game

The Football Trust,
Walkden House,
10 Melton Street,
London NW1 2EJ.

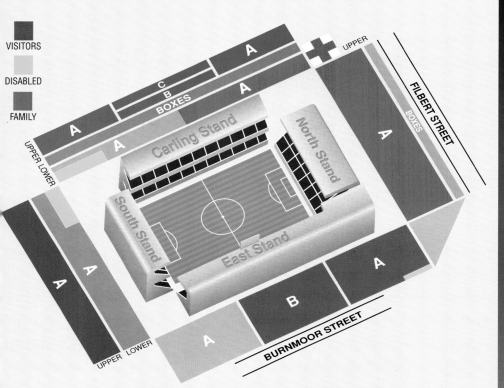

VISITORS
DISABLED
FAMILY

CARLING STAND
North Stand
South Stand
East Stand

UPPER
C
B
BOXES
A
A
A
UPPER
LOWER
A
A
A
A
A
B
A
A

FILBERT STREET
BOXES
BURNMOOR STREET
UPPER LOWER

MATCH DAY PRICES

Concession prices in brackets

CARLING STAND
Capacity 9,165

UPPER

Block A	£16 (8)
Block B	£20 (10)
Block C	£18 (9)

LOWER

Block A	£13

FAMILY

Block A	£13 (6)

NORTH STAND
Capacity 1,089

FAMILY

Block A	£12 (6)

EAST STAND
Capacity 2,950

SINGLE TIER

Block A	£12 (6)

VISITORS

Block A	£12 (8)
Block B	£15 (6)

SOUTH STAND
Capacity 8,600

UPPER

Block A	£15 (8)

LOWER

Block A	£12

FOOD AND DRINK

Bar

Tea/Coffee	0.90
Soft Drinks	1.00

Food

Quarter Pounder	1.60
Cheese Burger	1.80
Chicken Burger	1.80
Pies	1.40
Confectionery	0.60
Crisps	0.50
Popcorn	0.90

MISCELLANEOUS INFORMATION

Staged during matches:

Alan Birchenall's Half-Time Draws

Foxy Lady Cheerleaders

PROGRAMME: £2.00

GETTING THERE

Leicester City play at Filbert Street, south of Leicester City Centre. There is some street parking and a car park off Upperton Road as well as city centre car parks.

DIRECTIONS

From The North:
Exit M1 at Junction 22 heading for Leicester on the A50. Follow Leicester and city centre signs over five roundabouts for 6 miles until junction with Fosse Road North A5125. Turn right onto the A5125 for 1 mile then left onto the A47 King Richards Road. After half a mile turn right into Narborough Road North A46. After half a mile turn left onto Upperton Road, crossing the river and taking the first right for Filbert Street.

From The South:
Exit M1 at Junction 21 and head for Leicester on the A46. After half a mile take the second exit at the roundabout staying on the A46 Narborough Road. After Approximately 3 miles, turn right into Upperton Road, crossing the river and taking the first right for Filbert Street.

From The West:
Approaching on the M69, at Junction 21 with the M1, get onto the A46. Then as route for the South.

The main railway station is about one mile from the ground. No buses run directly to the ground so it is about a 20 minute walk.

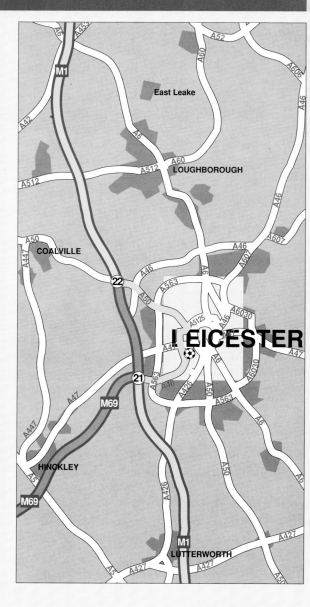

BBC Radio **Leicester**
Every day... not just *match* days!

1**☉**4.9FM

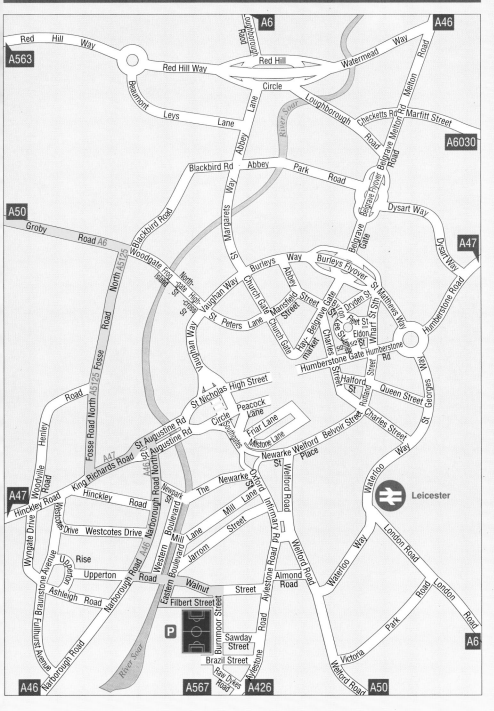

The best match in the world?

The best player in the world?

The best lager in the world? Probably.

Liverpool FC
Anfield Road
Liverpool
L4 0TH

Club Number: 0151·263·2361
Fax Number: 0151·260·8813
Tickets: 0151·260·8680

INFORMATION HOTLINES

ClubCall: 0891·12 11 84*

*Calls cost 49p per minute peak, 39p per minute off peak

CLUB SHOPS

LIVERWORLD
Liverpool Football Club
Opening Times:
Monday-Friday 9.00am-5.00pm
Match Saturdays: 9.00am-5.30pm (closed during game)
Match Sundays: 9.00am-Kick Off (plus 45 mins at end)
Match Evenings: 9.00am-Kick Off (plus 30 mins at end)
Tel: 0151·263·1760
Fax: 0151·264·9088
Mail Order Service: 0990·532532

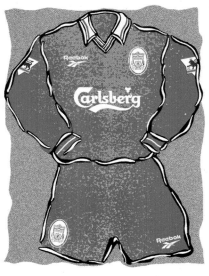

BOOKING INFORMATION

General Enquiries: 0151·260·8680
Credit Card Bookings: 0151·263·5727
Travel Club: 0151·260·8680
Recorded Information: 0151·260·9999

SPECIAL PACKAGES

RESTAURANT FACILITIES
Jim Kennefick: 0151·263·9199

STADIUM TOURS
Monday-Friday 10.30am-3.00pm
Bev Roberts: 0151·263·1433

CORPORATE HOSPITALITY/SPONSORSHIP
Jim Kennefick: 0151·263·9199

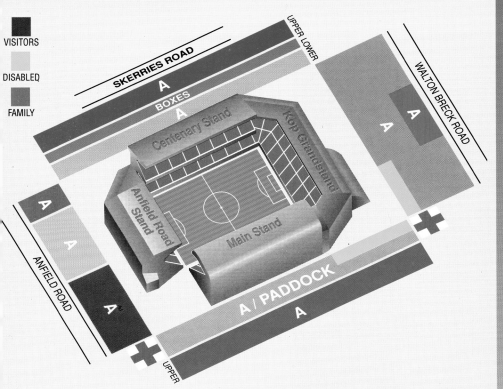

VISITORS
DISABLED
FAMILY

UPPER LOWER
SKERRIES ROAD
BOXES
A
A
Centenary Stand
Kop Grandstand
WALTON BRECK ROAD
A
A
Anfield Road Stand
Main Stand
A
A
A
ANFIELD ROAD
A
A / PADDOCK
A
UPPER

MATCH DAY PRICES

Concession prices in brackets

MAIN STAND
Capacity 8,152

UPPER	
Block A	£17

PADDOCK	
Block A	£17

ANFIELD ROAD
Capacity 5,512

LOWER	
Block A	£17

FAMILY	
Adult	£17
Child	£8.50

VISITORS	
Adult	£17
Child	£8.50

CENTENARY STAND
Capacity 11,410

UPPER	
Block A	£17

LOWER	
Block A	£17

KOP GRANDSTAND
Capacity 12,199

SINGLE TIER	
Block A	£14

FAMILY	
Adult	£14
Child	£7

FOOD AND DRINK

Bar

Beer	Bitter	1.50
	Lager	1.60
Tea/Coffee		0.95
Soft Drinks		1.20

Food

Pie/Pastie	1.20
Cheese & Onion Bap	1.00
Ham Baps	1.00
Sausage Rolls	0.90
Crisps	0.50

MISCELLANEOUS INFORMATION

Staged during matches:

DJ's playing the very latest chart music over the club Tannoys

PROGRAMME: £1.70

LIVERPOOL

Liverpool's Anfield Road ground is situated two miles north of Liverpool City Centre, close to Stanley Park. There is a sizeable car park by the Sports Centre in the park.

DIRECTIONS

From the North:
Approaching on the M6, exit at Junction 26 onto the M58 and continue until the end. At Junction 7 turn left onto the A59 Ormskirk Road. Continue on this road as it becomes Rice Lane, and cross over the roundabout into County Road. After ¼ mile turn left into Everton Valley and then right into Anfield Road. The ground is on the right.

From the South:
Approaching on the M6, exit at Junction 21a onto the M62. Exit the M62 at Junction 4 and get onto the A5080. At the junction with the A5058 turn right and continue along this road as it becomes Queens Drive. Continue to the junction with Walton Hall Avenue and turn left onto the A580 Walton Lane. Turn left into Anfield Road and the ground is on the right.

From the East:
Approaching on the M62 exit at Junction 4 and get onto the A5058. Then as route for the South.

Lime Street Railway Station is in the town centre, 2 miles from Anfield. Kirkdale Railway Station is 10 minutes walk from the ground.

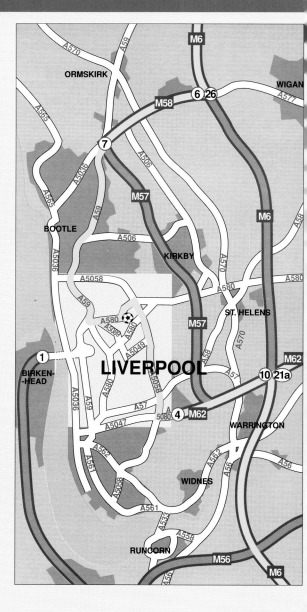

BBC Radio **Merseyside**
95.8FM 1485AM

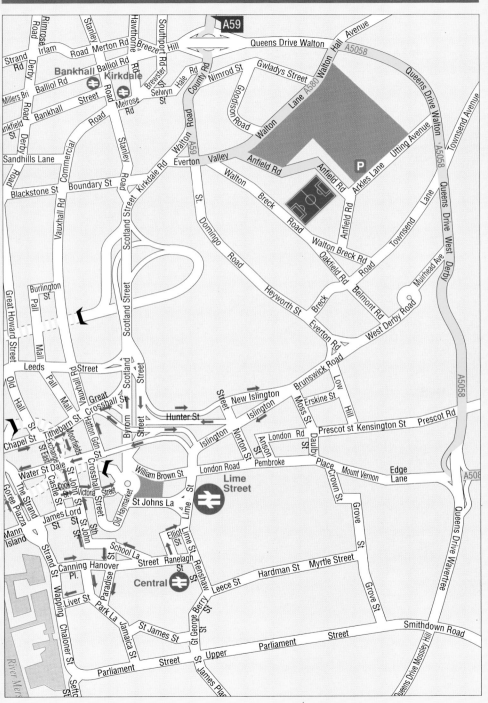

PICTURE *yourself*
WITH
A WINNER

SHARP
VIEW CAM

Sharp's latest winner is the revolutionary new **VIEWCAM** – the world's first fully integrated video camera, 8mm video deck and LCD colour monitor!

The **SHARP VIEWCAM** features a winning line-up of easy to use star attractions, for example, the LCD colour monitor means the end of "squinting" down a tiny viewfinder – you simply frame the subject or scene and press record!

The pivot between monitor and lens on the other hand offers total flexibility allowing low or high angle shots from almost any position. Swing the lens through 180 degrees to face the same way as the monitor and the **SHARP VIEWCAM** even lets you record yourself!

Replaying your action couldn't be easier either, as the LCD colour monitor delivers instant video playback with sound from the built in speaker – so family and friends can gather round and immediately share the fun.

SHARP
INTELLIGENT THINKING

SHARP ELECTRONICS (UK) LTD, SHARP HOUSE, THORP ROAD, NEWTON HEATH, MANCHESTER M40 5BE
For further information please call FREEPHONE 0800 262958

SHARP VIEWCAM · TV · VIDEO · AUDIO · MICROWAVE OVEN · COPIER · FAX · CALCULATOR · ELECTRONIC TYPEWRITER
ELECTRONIC IQ ORGANISER · NOTEBOOK PC · ELECTRONIC CASH REGISTER

Manchester United FC
Sir Matt Busby Way
Old Trafford
Manchester M16 0RA

Club Number: 0161·872·1661
Fax Number: 0161·876·5502
Tickets: 0161·872·0199

INFORMATION HOTLINES

ClubCall: 0891·12 11 61*

*Calls cost 49p per minute peak, 39p per minute off peak

CLUB SHOPS

MEGASTORE
21-26 United Road, Old Trafford
Opening Times:
Monday-Saturday: 9.00am-5.00pm
Match Saturdays: 9.00am-6.30pm
Sundays: 10.00am-4.00pm
Match Evenings: 9.00am-10.30pm
Tel: 0161·848·8181
Fax: 0161·877·1066
Mail Order Service: 0161·877·9777

SUPERSTORE
Sir Matt Busby Way
Opening Times:
Monday-Saturday: TBA
Match Saturdays: 9.00am-6.30pm
Match Sundays: 10.00am-6.30pm
Match Evenings: 4.00pm-10.30pm
Tel: 0161·848·8181
Mail Order Service: 0161·877·9777

BOOKING INFORMATION

General Enquiries: 0161·872·1661
Club General Enquiries: 0161·930·1968
Travel Club: 0161·872·5208
Recorded Info: 0161·872·0199

SPECIAL PACKAGES

RESTAURANT FACILITIES
Executive Department: 0161·872·3331

STADIUM TOURS
Museum & Tour Centre: 0161·877·4002

CORPORATE HOSPITALITY/SPONSORSHIP
Commercial Department: 0161·872·3488

MEMBERSHIP OFFICE
0161·872·5208

Rubbish weekend

Brilliant weekend

UMBRO®
The heart and soul
of football.™

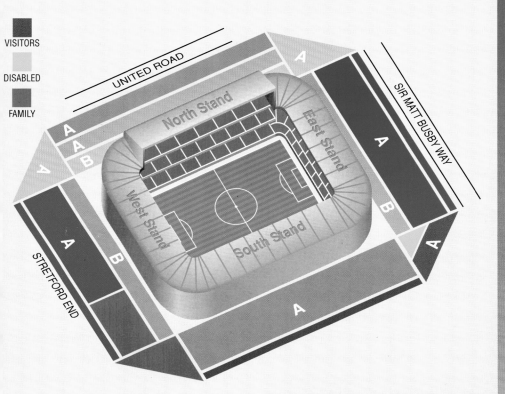

VISITORS

DISABLED

FAMILY

UNITED ROAD

North Stand

East Stand

West Stand

South Stand

SIR MATT BUSBY WAY

STRETFORD END

MATCH DAY PRICES

NORTH STAND
Capacity 26,084

UPPER	
Block A	£14

MIDDLE	
Block A	£16

LOWER	
Block A	£16
Block B	£18

SOUTH STAND
Capacity 10,183

LOWER	
Block A	£18

WEST STAND
Capacity 10,398

UPPER	
Block A	£16

LOWER	
Block A	£12

EAST STAND
Capacity 9,802

UPPER	
Block A	£16

LOWER	
Block B	£12

The prices quoted above apply to members. Add £2 to all of the above for non-members.

FOOD AND DRINK

Bar		
Beer	Lager	2.00
	Bitter	2.00
Cola		1.20
Juice		0.50
Coffee/Tea/Bovril		0.80

Food	
Pies/Pasties	1.10
Cheeseburger	1.70
M&M's	1.60
Chocolate Bar	0.50

MISCELLANEOUS INFORMATION

Manchester United's own radio station broadcasts direct from Old Trafford every match-day. Programmes include full match commentary, team interviews, traffic news, features for the partially sighted, and the very best in music. Frequency 1413AM

PROGRAMME: £1.50

73

GETTING THERE

Manchester United play at Old Trafford, two miles south-west of Manchester city centre. Parking is available at several paying car parks in the immediate vicinity of the ground.

DIRECTIONS

From The North:
Approaching on the M61, at Junction 1 continue onto the M602 and keep on this road for 4 miles. At Junction 3 turn right onto Trafford Road and after one mile turn right again into Trafford Park Road. Sir Matt Busby Way and Old Trafford are on the left.

From The South:
Take the M6 to Junction 19, turning onto the A556 Stockport Road which becomes the A56 at Altrincham. This becomes the Chester Road. After 9 miles, turn left onto the the A5063 Trafford Road, left onto the A5081 Trafford Park Road and left again into Sir Matt Busby Way. Old Trafford is on the right.

From The West:
Approaching on the M62, at Junction 12 continue on the M602, keeping to this road for 4 miles. Then as route for North.

From The East:
Get onto the M63 and at Junction 7 turn onto the A556. Then as route for South.

The nearest Metrolink stations are Old Trafford and Trafford Bar.

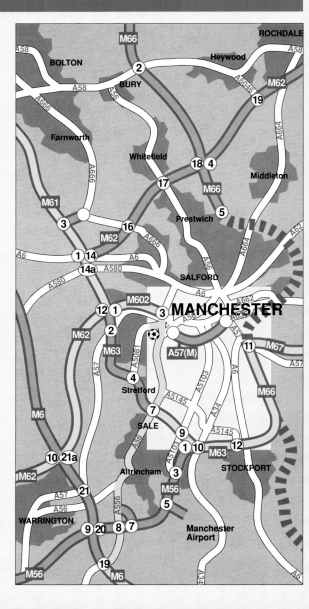

MANCHESTER UNITED RADIO

1413 AM

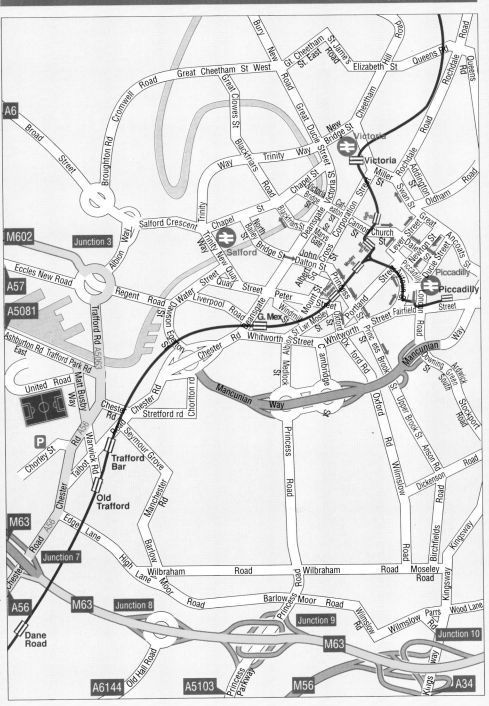

BORO'S
INTERNATIONALS
WILL BE
BRANDED
SKILLFUL,
DAZZLING,
INSPIRATIONAL...
AND CELLNET.

We're proud to have the Cellnet name emblazoned on the players' shirts. And, like Boro, we provide a truly worldwide coverage. With Cellnet, you can make and receive calls across the UK and in over 40 countries around the world. We're delighted that our continued sponsorship of Boro helps to bring a more international flavour to the Cellnet Riverside Stadium. Together with Boro, we'll make a winning team for 1996/97.

CELLNET AND BORO. A TEAM WORTH SHOUTING ABOUT.
To find out more about connecting to the net, call us on 0800 21 4000.

Middlesbrough FC
Cellnet Riverside Stadium
Middlesbrough
Cleveland TS3 6RS

Club Number: 01642·227227
Fax Number: 01642·207098
Tickets: 01642·207014

INFORMATION HOTLINES

Boro Livewire   0891·42 42 00*
*Calls cost 49p per minute peak, 39p per minute off peak

CLUB SHOPS

BORO CLUB SHOP
Cellnet Riverside Stadium
Opening Times:
Monday-Friday: 9.30am-5pm
Match Saturdays: 10.00am-2.30pm, 5.00pm-6.00pm
Match Sundays: 12.00am-4.00pm
Match Evenings: 9.30am-7.30pm
Sundays: 11.00am-3.30pm
Tel: 01642·207005
Fax: 01642·248450
Mail Order Service: 01642·454522

BOOKING INFORMATION

General Enquiries: 01642·207014
Credit Card Bookings: 01642·207014
Travel Club: 01642·207016

SPECIAL PACKAGES

RESTAURANT FACILITIES
01642·227227

STADIUM TOURS
Tuesday/Thursday/Sunday: 01642·207040

CORPORATE HOSPITALITY
Packages from £1,000
Helen Coverdale: 01642·227227

SPONSORSHIP/MATCH BALL
Packages from £500
Helen Coverdale: 01642·227227

THE ULTIMATE IN SPORTS AND LEISURE WEAR

OFFICIAL KIT SUPPLIER TO
MIDDLESBROUGH FOOTBALL CLUB

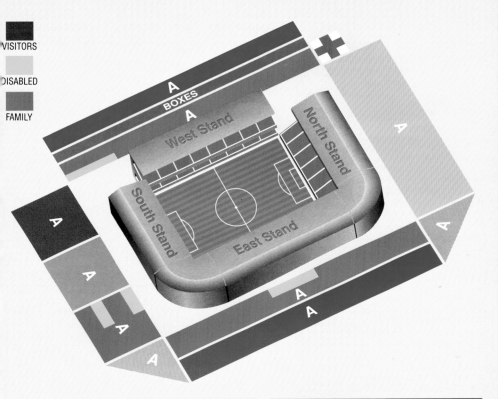

VISITORS

DISABLED

FAMILY

MATCH DAY PRICES

Concession prices in brackets

WEST STAND
Capacity 8,995

UPPER
Block A   £19

FAMILY
Block A £15 (7.50)

SOUTH STAND
Capacity 6,900

SINGLE TIER
Block A 12.50 (7.50)

FAMILY
Block A 12.50 (7.50)

VISITORS
Block A   £17 (10)

NORTH STAND
Capacity 7,030

SINGLE TIER
Block A 12.50 (7.50)

EAST STAND
Capacity 7,193

SINGLE TIER
Block A 17.50 (12.50)

CORNERS
Block A 12.50 (7.50)

FAMILY
Block A £15 (7.50)

FOOD AND DRINK

Bar

Beer	Bitter	1.70
	Lager	1.80
Hot Drinks		0.80
Soft Drinks		0.90

Food

Burgers	1.70
Hot Dogs	1.60
Pies	1.00
Chicken Burgers	1.80
Sausage Roll	0.80
Chips	1.00
Mars/Twix/Snickers	0.50

MISCELLANEOUS INFORMATION

Boro TV, with action of previous games with the day's opposition, is shown in the stadium concourses an hour and a half before each game.

PROGRAMME: £1.50

MIDDLESBROUGH

GETTING THERE

Middlesbrough is based in the Cellnet Riverside Stadium in the Middlehaven development area, 15 minutes walk from the town centre.

DIRECTIONS

From The North:
Approaching Middlesbrough on the A19, cross over the River Tees. Turn left onto the A66 Middlesbrough bypass, continuing for 3 miles until the first roundabout. Turn left into Forest Road and the ground is straight ahead.

From The South:
Approaching from the South on the M1, exit where signposted to Teeside onto the A19. After 30 miles turn right onto the A66 Middlesbrough bypass. Then as route for North.

From The West:
From the A1(M) exit at Junction 57 onto the A66(M), following it until the end, turning onto the A66. Continue straight on the A66 for approximately 20 miles, turning left at the roundabout into Forest Road. The ground is straight ahead.

Middlesbrough Station is located on Albert Road, ten minutes walk from the ground.

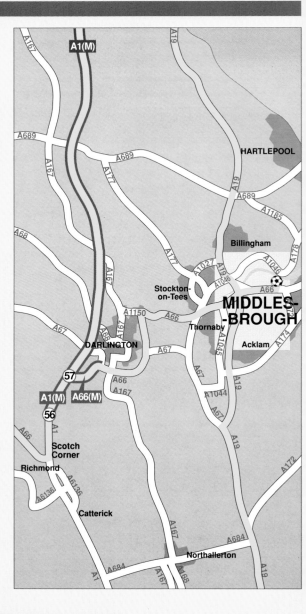

THE REVOLUTION CONTINUES

Exclusively on 100.7FM

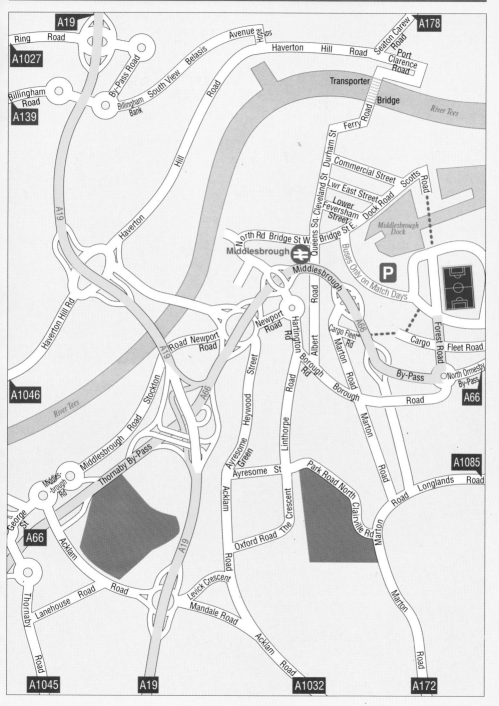

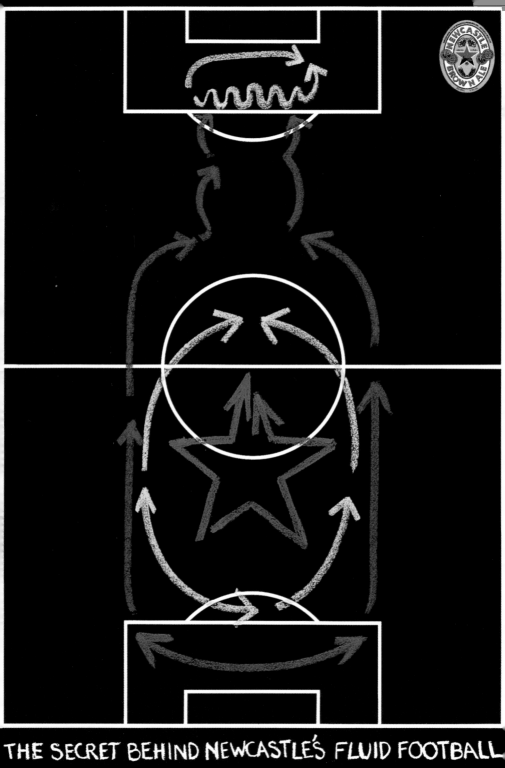

THE SECRET BEHIND NEWCASTLE'S FLUID FOOTBALL

Newcastle United FC
St James' Park
Newcastle-Upon-Tyne
NE1 4ST

Club Number: 0191·201·8400
Fax Number: 0191·201·8600
Tickets: 0191·261·1571

INFORMATION HOTLINES

ClubCall: 0891·12 11 90*
Information: 0891·12 15 90*

*Calls cost 49p per minute peak, 39p per minute off peak

CLUB SHOPS

NEWCASTLE UNITED OFFICIAL STORE
St James' Park
Opening Times:
Monday-Friday: 9.00am-5.00pm
Match Saturdays: 9.00am-6.00pm
Match Sundays: 9.00am-6.00pm
Match Evenings: 9.00am-10.00pm
Tel: 0191·201·8426
Fax: 0191·201·8605
Mail Order Service: 0191·262·6878

NEWCASTLE UNITED OFFICIAL STORE
Monument Mall, Newcastle-Upon-Tyne
Opening Times:
Monday-Friday: 9.00am-5.30pm, 9.00am-8.00pm Thursday
Match Saturdays: 9.00am-6.00pm
Match Sundays: 11.00am-5.00pm (From 4/10/96)
Match Evenings: 9.00am-5.30pm
Tel: 0191·232·4488
Mail Order Service: 0191·262·6878

BOOKING INFORMATION

General Enquiries: 0191·261·1571
Credit Card Bookings: 0191·261·1571
Travel Club: 0191·201·8550

SPECIAL PACKAGES

RESTAURANT FACILITIES
0191·201·8439

STADIUM TOURS
0191·261·1571

**CORPORATE HOSPITALITY/SPONSORSHIP/
MATCH BALL**
Trevor Garwood: 0191·201·8422

Stars and Stripes
a winning combination

adidas
OFFICIAL SUPPLIERS OF KIT
AND TRAINING WEAR TO
NEWCASTLE F.C.

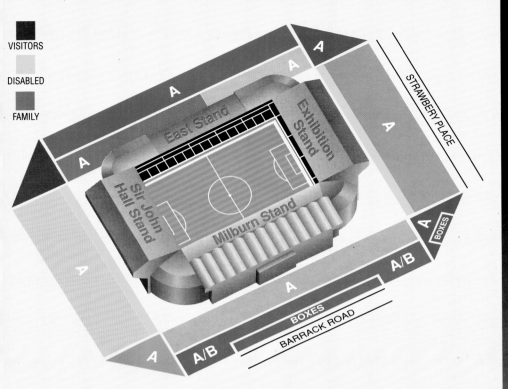

VISITORS

DISABLED

FAMILY

MATCH DAY PRICES

Adult Season ticket prices are shown below

EAST STAND
Capacity 4,941

UPPER
Block A	£389

LOWER
Block A	£278

FAMILY
Block A	£250

EXHIBITION STAND
Capacity 11,872

SINGLE TIER
Block A	£320
Disabled	£160

CORNERS
Block A	£320

MILBURN STAND
Capacity 8,713

UPPER
Block A	£347
Block B	£416

LOWER
Block A	£391

SIR JOHN HALL
Capacity 11,037

SINGLE TIER
Block A	£320
Disabled	£160

CORNER
Corner A	£320

FOOD AND DRINK

Bar
Beer	Lager	2.00
	Bitter	1.90
Tea/Coffee		0.90
Soft Drinks		1.00

Food
Hamburger	1.80
Hot Dog	1.80
Pies/Pasties	1.20
Chips	0.90
Chicken Burger	2.00

MISCELLANEOUS INFORMATION

TV highlights before and after games in concourses

Monthly magazine £2.50

PROGRAMME: £1.50

GETTING THERE

Newcastle United play at St James' Park, half a mile from Newcastle city centre. The metro system is very efficient and there is a station by the ground. Some car parking is available on Barrack Road.

DIRECTIONS

From the North:
Exit A1 onto the A167 Ponteland Road heading toward the city centre. At the fourth roundabout after approximately 1½ miles, turn left onto Jedburgh Road. Take the first exit, turning right onto Grandstand Road and then left onto the A189 Ponteland Road. Keep on this road which becomes Barrack Road until the roundabout. The ground is on the left.

From the South:
From the A1(M) turn off at the junction with the A1 and continue on the A1 until the junction with the A184. Turn onto the the A184 and continue along this road, bearing left onto the A189. Continue over the River Tyne on the Redheugh Bridge, go straight over the roundabout onto Blenheim Street and continue until you meet Bath Lane. Turn left into Bath Lane, right into Corporation Street, and left at the roundabout into Gallowgate. At the next roundabout Barrack Road and the ground are straight ahead.

Newcastle Central Railway Station is half a mile from St James' park. The metro runs every 3-4 minutes to St James' Station.

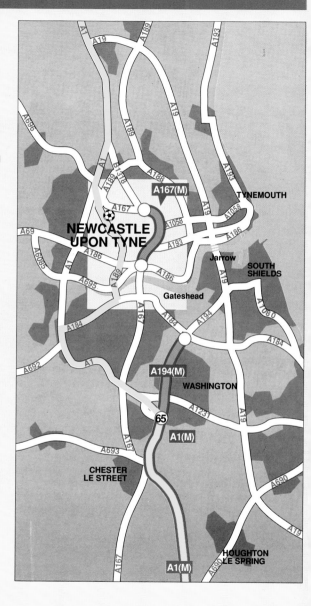

Tune Army
Saturdays 2 - 5.15pm

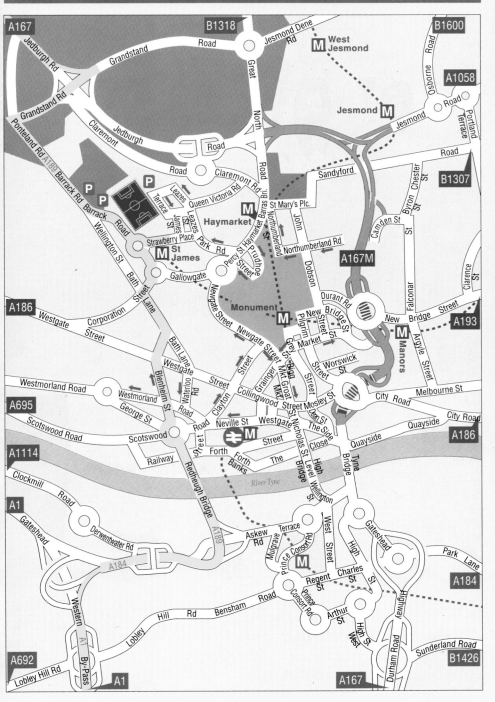

NEWCASTLE UNITED

87

IT'S GREAT TO HAVE A CANADIAN ON YOUR SIDE.

Labatt's are proud to sponsor Nottingham Forest Football Club.

Labatt's™
Canadian Lager

Nottingham Forest FC
City Ground
Nottingham
NG2 5FJ

Club Number: 0115·952·6000
Fax Number: 0115·952·6003
Tickets: 0115·952·6002

INFORMATION HOTLINES

ClubCall: 0891·12 11 74*

*Calls cost 49p per minute peak, 39p per minute off peak

CLUB SHOPS

SOUVENIR SHOP
City Ground Stadium
Opening Times:
Monday-Friday: 9.00am-5.00pm
Match Saturdays: 9.00am-5.30pm (Closed during game)
Match Sundays: 10.00am-Half hour after game
Match Evenings: 9.00am-Half hour after game
Tel: 0115·952·6026
Fax: 0115·952·6007
Mail Order Service: 0115·952·6026

BOOKING INFORMATION

General Enquiries:	0115·952·6002
Credit Card Bookings:	0115·971·8181
Travel Club:	0115·952·6002
Recorded Information:	0115·952·6016

SPECIAL PACKAGES

RESTAURANT FACILITIES
0115·952·6015

STADIUM TOURS
Community: 0115·952·6001

CORPORATE HOSPITALITY/SPONSORSHIP/
MATCH BALL
Commercial Office: 0115·952·6006

JUNIOR REDS
0115·952·6001

THE 'PITCH SPORTS DINER'
0115·952·6666

2nd: Sex
3rd: Money

UMBRO®
The heart and soul
of football.™

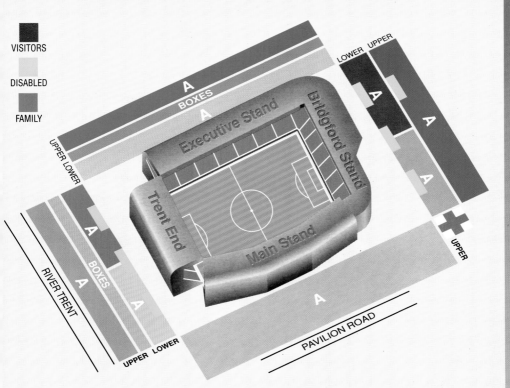

VISITORS

DISABLED

FAMILY

MATCH DAY PRICES

Concession prices in brackets

EXECUTIVE STAND
Capacity 9,788

UPPER

Block A	£19

LOWER

Block A	£18

BRIDGFORD STAND
Capacity 7,710

UPPER

Block A	£19

LOWER

Block A	£19

VISITORS

Block A	£19

WEST STAND
Capacity 5,708

SINGLE TIER

Block A	£20

TREND END
Capacity 6,770

UPPER

Block A	£19

LOWER

Block A	£18

FAMILY

Block A	£18

FOOD AND DRINK

Bar

Tea/Coffee/Bovril	0.90
Cold Drinks (16oz)	0.90

Food

Hamburger	1.70
Cheeseburger	1.80
Hot Dog	1.60
Pies	1.30
Soup	0.90
Mars/Twix/Snickers	0.30

MISCELLANEOUS INFORMATION

Chart music over Tannoy

Competitions

Half-time Premier score round-up

PROGRAMME: £1.50

GETTING THERE

Nottingham Forest play at the City Ground, south of the city centre and the River Trent. Parking prohibitions are in force on match days but the council operates a paying car park on Victora Embankment - a 15 minute walk away.

DIRECTIONS

From The North:
Exit M1 at Junction 26 heading for Nottingham on the A610. Stay on the A610 to the city centre, a distance of approximately 6 miles, and follow the one way system onto Lower Parliament Street heading for the A60 London Road. Once on this road, cross the River Trent, turning into Pavilion Road for the City Ground.

From The South:
Exit M1 at Junction 24 heading for Nottingham South on the A453. After approximately 7 miles keep to the left, avoiding the fly-over, and at the roundabout take the left exit to pass under the A52 onto the B679 Wilford Lane. Go to the end, turn left onto the A60, right onto Radcliffe Road and left into Colwick Road for the City Ground.

From The East:
Take the A52 until the roundabout with the A6011 Radcliffe Road, keeping left when road splits and turning right into Colwick Road for the City Ground.

Nottingham Midland Railway Station is situated in the town centre, approximately half a mile from the ground.

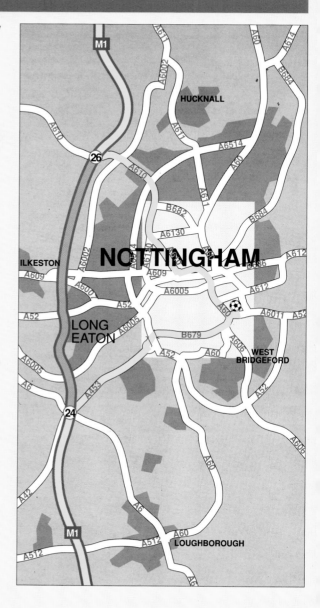

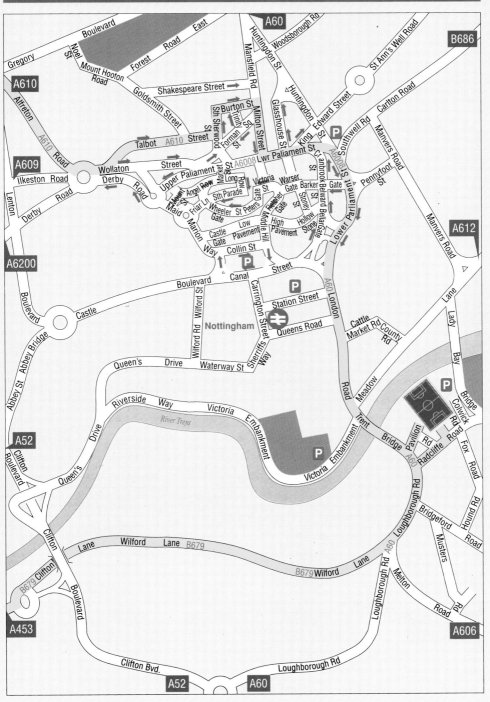

93

WINNING COMPUTER SOLUTIONS

Sanderson Electronics PLC is a leading supplier of premier computer solutions, is listed on the London Stock Exchange and employs more than 700 people in 25 office locations throughout the United Kingdom, Australia, New Zealand and East Asia. Sanderson has an extensive portfolio of application software packages which operate on a wide variety of hardware platforms under open system environments such as UNIX and DOS. Sanderson is committed to providing its 4000 customers with reliable products of a high quality and with a high standard of service and support.

1   **Manufacturin**
2   **Solicitors**
3   **Credit Management**
4   **Finance and Distribution**
5   **Supply Chain Management**
6   **Police**
7   **Direct Marketing**
8   **Local Government**
9   **Airports**
10   **Insurance**
11   **Printing Industry**
12   **Healthcare**
13   **Computer Based Training**
14   **Schools and Colleges**
15   **Hotels**
16   **Production Monitoring**
17   **Processing Industry**
18   **Media and Publishing**

 SANDERSO

For Premier Computer Solutions

Sheffield Wednesday FC
Penistone Road
Hillsborough
Sheffield S6 1SW

Club Number: **0114·234·3122**
Fax Number: **0114·233·7145**
Tickets: **0114·233·7233**

INFORMATION HOTLINES

ClubCall: **0891·12 11 86***
*Calls cost 49p per minute peak, 39p per minute off peak

CLUB SHOPS

THE OWLS SUPERSTORE
Hillsborough, Sheffield
Opening Times:
Monday-Friday: 9.00am-5.00pm
Match Saturdays: 9.00am-6.00pm, except match
Match Sundays: 9.00am-6.30pm, except match
Match Evenings: 9.00am-10.30pm, except match
Tel: 0114·234·3342
Fax: 0114·285·1443
Mail Order Service: 0114·234·3342

WEDNESDAY GEAR
Orchard Square Shopping Centre, Sheffield
Opening Times:
Monday-Friday: 9.00am-5.30pm
Match Saturdays: 9.00am-5.30pm
Match Sundays: Closed
Match Evenings: 9.00am-5.30pm
Tel: 0114·275·1443

BOOKING INFORMATION

General Enquiries: 0114·234·3122
Credit Card Bookings: 0114·234·3122
Travel Club: 0114·234·9906
Recorded Info: 0114·234·3122

SPECIAL PACKAGES

RESTAURANT FACILITIES
0114·233·3289

STADIUM TOURS
Community Programme: 0114·233·3262

CORPORATE HOSPITALITY
Delegate Rate: £2250
0114·233·3289

SPONSORSHIP
Sean O'Toole
0114·233·7235

THREE SHIRTS ON A LINE.

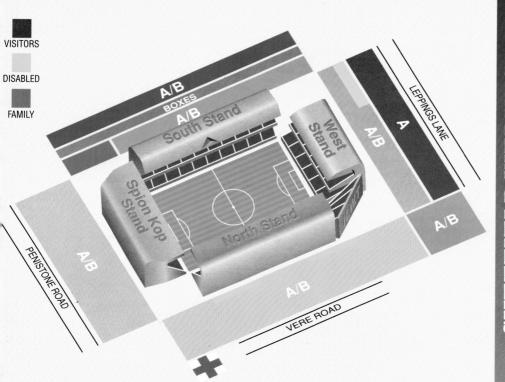

VISITORS

DISABLED

FAMILY

MATCH DAY PRICES

Concession prices in brackets

NORTH STAND
Capacity 9,000

SINGLE TIER

A Premier £18 (12)
B Standard £13 (9)

N. WEST TERRACE
Capacity 1,300

CORNER

A Premier £10 (6)
B Standard £6 (4.50)

WEST STAND
Capacity 6,500

VISITORS

Block A £13 (9)

LOWER

A Premier £10 (6)
B Standard £8 (4.50)

SOUTH STAND
Capacity 8,000

UPPER

A Premier £18 (12)
B Standard £13 (9)

LOWER

A Premier £18 (12)
B Standard £13 (9)

FAMILY

Block A 10.50 (6.50)

SPION KOP
Capacity 11,000

SINGLE TIER

A Premier £12 (7)
B Standard £9 (5.50)

FOOD AND DRINK

Bar

Tea/Coffee	0.90
Hot Chocolate	0.90
Soft Drinks	1.40

Food

Hot Dog	1.50
Pies	1.30
Cheese and Onion Pastie	1.30
Sausage Roll	1.10
Chips	0.90
Confectionery	0.60

MISCELLANEOUS INFORMATION

Staged during game:

**Puma Penalty Competition:
Lucky supporter from the crowd gets
chance to win £250 of Puma
sportswear.**

PROGRAMME: £1.50

GETTING THERE

Sheffield Wednesday's stadium is situated 2 miles from the city centre. All visitors are advised to approach via the M1/A61 route and avoid the city centre. Parking is possible in the area just north of Hillsborough around Doe Royd Lane as well as next to the stadium.

DIRECTIONS

All Routes:
Approaching on the M1, exit at Junction 36 onto the A61. Keep on this road for 7 miles, crossing over the roundabout onto Pennistone Road. The ground is on the right and some parking in Parkside Road.

Sheffield Railway Station is situated in the town centre, approximately 2 miles from the ground. Buses run to the ground from nearby Pond Street.

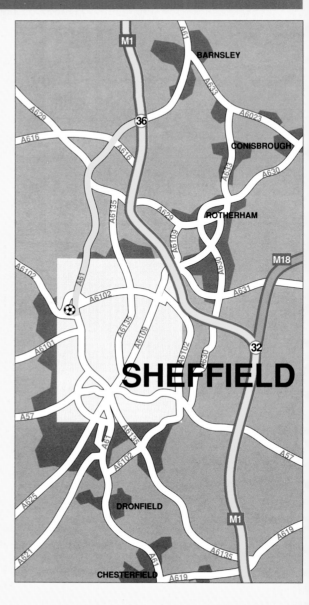

SHEFFIELD WEDNESDAY

Lyminster Rd
Pennistone Rd North
A61
Doe Royd Ln
A6135
Barnsley Road
Meadow Bank Rd
A6109
M1
Junction 34
Meadow Hall Road
Leppings Lane
Vere Road
Herries Rd
Herries Road
Herries Rd South
Herries Road
Middlewood
Pennistone Rd A61/Pennistone
Parkside Rd
Road
Shircliffe Rd
Cooks Wood Road
Owler St
Upwell St
Brightside La
Hawke St
Janson St
Sheffield Road
Common
Broughton Lane
A6102
A6102
Bradfield Road
Road
Rutland Rd
Barnsley Road
Saville St
East
Attercliffe
Rd
Holme Ln
Langsett Rd
A6101
Rutland Rd
Pennistone Road
Neepsend Lane
Mowbray St
Burngrave Road
Wicker
Saville Street
Spital Hill
Langsett Rd Infirmary Road
Nursery
Shales Moor
Moor
Hoyle St
Gibralter West Fields St
Bak
Corporation St
River Don
Street
Blonk St
West Bar
Bridge St
Castle Gate
Park Square
Sheffield Parkway
A57
Meadow St
Scotland St
Netherthorpe Rd
Tenter Street
West Bar Green St
Queen St
Nth Church St
Bank
Sing Hill Angel St
Castle
Hay-market
Sheffield
Hill
Broad Lane
Townhead St
Campo La
Church St High
St
Gate
St
Commercial St
Pond
Broad
West
Glossop Road
Upper Hanover St
Rockingham Street
Leopold St
Church St
Pinstone St
Howard St
Street
Sheaf St
Duke Street
A57
Western Bank
Brook
Witham Rd
Glossop Road
Road
Clarkehouse Road
Moore
Charter Row
Furnival Gate
The Moor
Furnival Square
Furnival St
Arundel Gate
Brown Paternoster Row
Shoreham St
Talbot St
A616
Street
St. Mary's Gate
Eyre Street
Matilda Street
Shoreham St
Suffolk Road
Shrewsbury Road
Ecclesall Road
Bramall La
Shoreham St
St. Mary's Road
Queens Rd
Granville Road
A625
A621
A61

LEADING PLAYERS IN THE FIELD

Sanderson Electronics PLC is a leading supplier of premier computer solutions, is listed on the London Stock Exchange and employs more than 700 people in 25 office locations throughout the United Kingdom, Australia, New Zealand and East Asia. Sanderson has an extensive portfolio of application software packages which operate on a wide variety of hardware platforms under open system environments such as UNIX and DOS. Sanderson is committed to providing its 4000 customers with reliable products of a high quality and with a high standard of service and support.

1   Manufacturing
2   Solicitors
3   Credit Management
4   Finance and Distribution
5   Supply Chain Management
6   Police
7   Direct Marketing
8   Local Government
9   Airports
10   Insurance
11   Printing Industry
12   Healthcare
13   Computer Based Training
14   Schools and Colleges
15   Hotels
16   Production Monitoring
17   Processing Industry
18   Media and Publishing

SANDERSON

For Premier Computer Solutions

Southampton FC
The Dell
Milton Road
Southampton SO15 2XH

Club Number: 01703·220505
Fax Number: 01703·330360
Tickets: 01703·228575

INFORMATION HOTLINES

ClubCall: **0891·12 11 78***

*Calls cost 49p per minute peak, 39p per minute off peak

CLUB SHOPS

SAINTS SOCCER SHOP
145 Milton Road. Southampton
Opening Times:
Monday-Friday: 9.30am-5.00pm
Match Saturdays: 9.30am-5.00pm
Match Sundays: 2.00pm-6.00pm
Match Evenings: 9.30am-10.00pm
Tel: 01703·236400
Fax: 01703·236300
Mail Order Service: 01703·236400

BOOKING INFORMATION

General Enquiries: 01703·220505
Credit Card Bookings: 01703·337171
Travel Club: 01703·334172
Recorded Info: 01703·228575

SPECIAL PACKAGES

STADIUM TOURS
Community Department: 01703·334172

CORPORATE HOSPITALITY/SPONSORSHIP/
MATCH BALL
Kim Lawford: 01703·331417

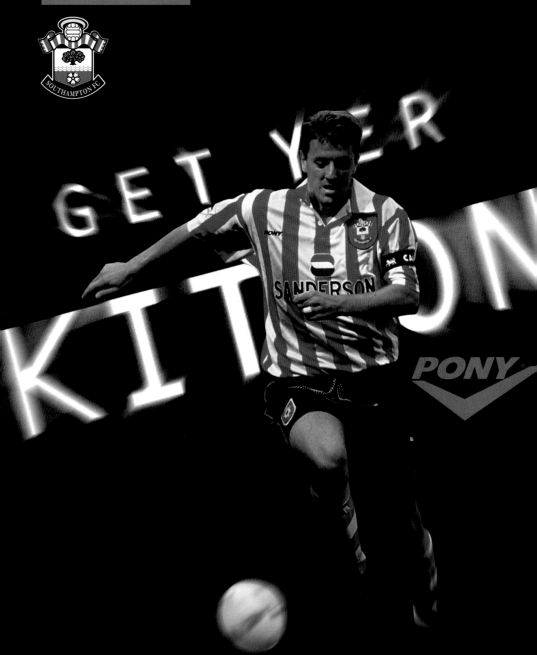

Official Southampton F.C.
kit and training wear

Available in store now.

GET YER
KIT ON

PONY

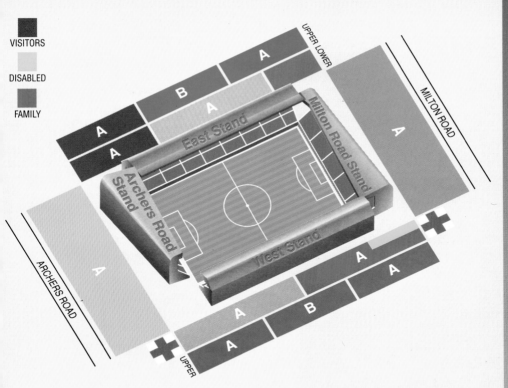

VISITORS

DISABLED

FAMILY

UPPER LOWER

MILTON ROAD

East Stand

Milton Road Stand

Archers Road Stand

West Stand

ARCHERS ROAD

A B A A A A B A A A A B A A

UPPER

SOUTHAMPTON

MATCH DAY PRICES

Concession prices in brackets

WEST STAND

Capacity 6,074

UPPER	
Block A	£17
Block B	£18

LOWER	
Block A	£15 (6)

FAMILY	
Block A	£14 (6)

ARCHERS ROAD

Capacity 1,299

SINGLE TIER	
Block A	£17 (6)

EAST STAND

Capacity 4,882

UPPER	
Block A	£17
Block B	£18

LOWER	
Block A	£15 (6)

VISITORS	
Block A	£17

MILTON ROAD

Capacity 2,897

SINGLE TIER	
Block A	£17 (6)

FOOD AND DRINK

Bar

Tea	0.60
Coffee	0.70
Soft Drinks	0.95

Food

Jumbo Hot Dog	1.80
Quarter Pounder	1.80
Cheeseburger	1.95
Pies/Pasties	1.35
Sausage Rolls	0.90
Mars/Twix	0.60

MISCELLANEOUS INFORMATION

PRE MATCH ENTERTAINMENT

Provided by local radio BBC Radio Solent. Includes interviews with players & music etc.

PROGRAMME: £1.50

103

GETTING THERE

Southampton play at the Dell, situated half a mile from the city centre. It is usually possible to park near the ground.

DIRECTIONS

From The North:
Follow the M3 to the end exiting at Junction 4 onto The Avenue (A33). After 2½ miles turn right into Northlands Road. Follow to the end T-junction with Archers Road. The Dell is opposite.

From The West:
From the M27 exit at Junction 3, turning right onto the M271. After 1½ miles turn left at the roundabout onto the A3024, going over the flyover and turning left after approximately 2 miles into Central Station Bridge. Turn right at the roundabout into Commercial Road, left into Hill Lane and after approximately half a mile right into Archers Road. The Dell is on the right.

From The East:
From the M27 exit at Junction 5 left onto the Swaythling Link Road and on onto the High Road. Turn right where the road divides onto the A35 Burgess Road for 1 mile. Turn left onto The Avenue and right into Northlands Road. Follow to the end T-junction with Archers Road. The Dell is opposite.

Southampton Central Railway Station is a ten minute walk to the ground.

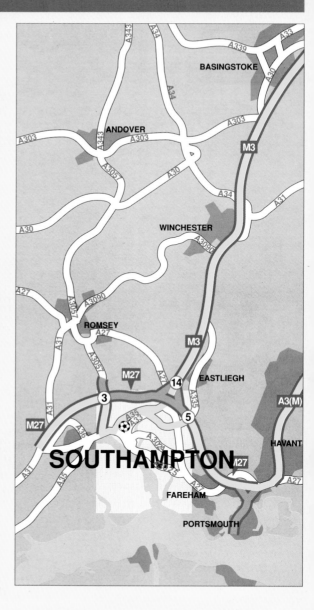

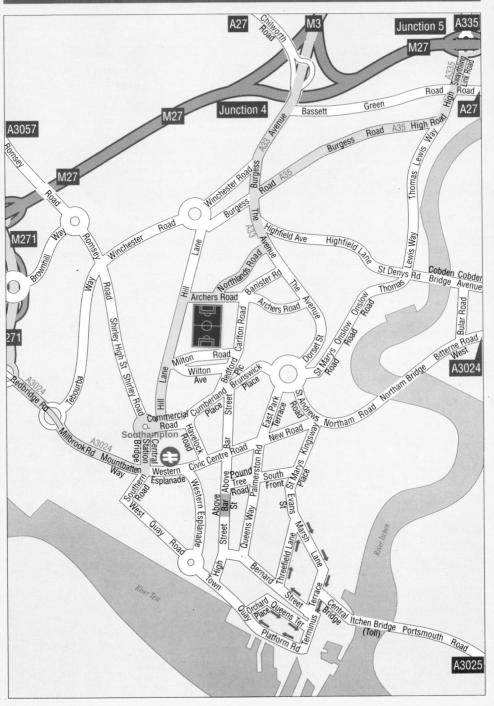

The best
uncapped player
in the league.

Sunderland AFC
Roker Park
Grantham Road
Sunderland SR6 9SW

Club Number: 0191·514·0332
Fax Number: 0191·514·5854
Tickets: 0191·564·2596

INFORMATION HOTLINES

ClubCall: 0891·12 11 40*

*Calls cost 49p per minute peak, 39p per minute off peak

CLUB SHOPS

SHOP ON THE PARK
Roker Park, Sunderland
Opening Times:
Monday-Friday: 9.00am-5.00pm
Match Saturdays: 9.30am-5.00pm, except match
Match Sundays: 9.30am-5.00pm, except match
Match Evenings: 9.30am-Kick Off, plus 30 minutes at end
Tel: 0191·510·2642
Fax: 0191·514·5854
Mail Order Service: 0191·385·2778
Mail Order Fax: 0191·385·2811

SHOP 2
10 Market Square, Sunderland
Opening Times
Monday-Friday: 9.00am-5.00pm
Match Saturdays: 9.00am-5.00pm
Sun Matches: Closed
Match Eves: Closed
Tel: 0191·564·0002

BOOKING INFORMATION

General Enquiries:	0191·514·0332
Credit Card Bookings:	0191·564·2596
Travel Club:	0191·514·0332
Football in the Community	0191·510·9111

SPECIAL PACKAGES

RESTAURANT FACILITIES
0191·514·0332

STADIUM TOURS
Kerry Smith: 0191·514·0332

**CORPORATE HOSPITALITY/SPONSORSHIP/
MATCH BALL**
Cathy Kerr: 0191·514·0332

IN THE HEAT OF THE PREMIERSHIP

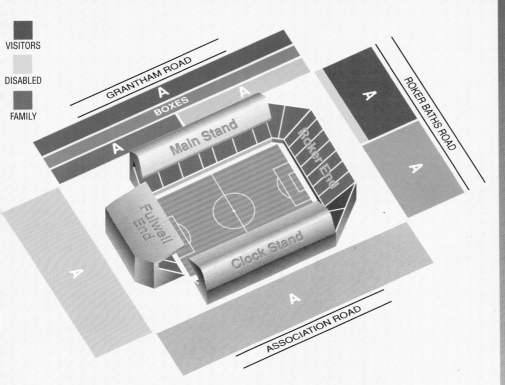

VISITORS

DISABLED

FAMILY

MATCH DAY PRICES

MAIN STAND

UPPER

Standing A   £16

LOWER

Standing A   £16

FAMILY

Standing A   £16

ROKER END

SINGLE TIER

Standing A   £16

VISITORS

Standing A   £16

CLOCK STAND

SINGLE TIER

Block A	£19
Block B	£22
Standing C	£16

FULWELL END

SINGLE TIER

Standing A   £16

FOOD AND DRINK

Bar

Tea/Coffees/Bovril	0.50
Soft Drinks	0.50

Food

Pies and Pasties	0.90
Hamburgers	0.85
Hot Dogs	0.75
Crisps	0.30

MISCELLANEOUS INFORMATION

Sunderland's new stadium is due for completion in time for the 1997/98 season. Its capacity of 34,000 can be easily increased to 40,000. There is a Visitors' Centre for people wishing to see how the work is progressing. Telephone: 0191·567·1177.

PROGRAMME: £1.50

GETTING THERE

Sunderland play at Roker Park, an old ground with a large amount of uncovered standing room. This situation will be improved when they move to their new gound next season. There is ample parking in the local streets around the ground.

DIRECTIONS

From The South:

Exit the A1 at Junction 64 which is signposted to Washington, Birtley A195. Get onto the Western Highway. At the roundabout, after 1½ miles, follow the signs to Sunderland A1231 onto the Washington Highway. Take the second exit onto the A1231 and stay on the A1231 for 4½ miles heading for the city centre. Follow the signs to Roker and get onto the Queens Road B1289. After 1 mile, the traffic enters the one way system. Follow the signs to Roker.

Seaburn Railway Station is a 10 minute walk from the ground.

Roker Roar
Saturdays 2 - 5.15pm

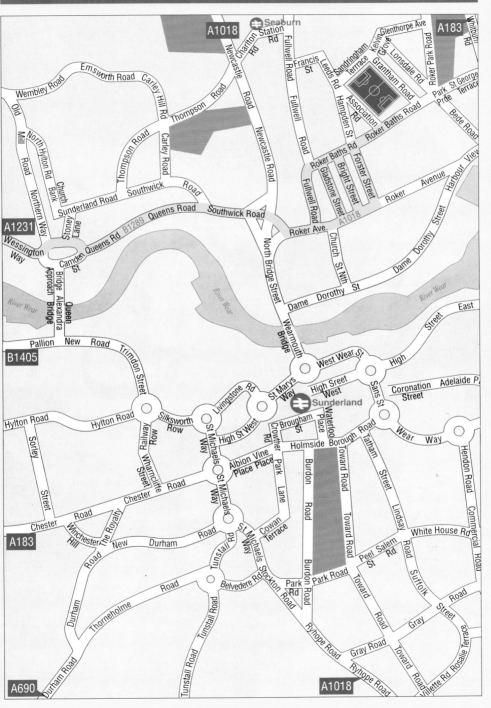

Official Tottenham Hotspur F.C.
kit and training wear

Available in store now.

Tottenham Hotspur FC
748 High Road
Tottenham
London N17 0AP

Club Number: 0181·365·5000
Fax Number: 0181·365·5005
Tickets: 0181·365·5050
Members: 0181·365·5100
Non-Members: 0181·396·4567

INFORMATION HOTLINES

Spursline: 0891·33 55 55*
Information: 0891·33 55 66*

*Calls cost 49p per minute peak, 39p per minute off peak

CLUB SHOPS

SPURS SHOP
1/3 Park Lane, Tottenham
Opening Times:
Monday-Friday: 9.30am-5.30pm
Match Saturdays: 9.30am-3.00pm, 4.45pm-6.00pm
Match Sundays: 11.00am-4.00pm, 5.45pm-6.30pm
Match Evenings: 9.30am-7.45pm, 9.45pm-10.15pm
Tel: 0181·365·5042
Mail Order Service: 0181·808·5959

SPURS SPORTSWEAR
766 High Road, Tottenham
Opening Times:
Monday-Friday: 9.30am-5.30pm
Match Saturdays: 9.30am-3.00pm, 4.45pm-6.00pm
Match Sundays: 11.00am-4.00pm, 5.45pm-6.30pm
Match Evenings: 9.30am-7.45pm, 9.45pm-10.15pm
Tel: 0181·365·5041
Mail Order Service: 0181·808·5959

BOOKING INFORMATION

General Enquiries: 0181·365·5050
Credit Cards (Members): 0181·365·5100
Credit Cards (Non-Members) 0171·396·4567
Travel Club: (Members) 0181·365·5150

SPECIAL PACKAGES

STADIUM TOURS
Main Reception: 0181·365·5000

CORPORATE HOSPITALITY/SPONSORSHIP/
MATCH BALL/MATCH ENTERTAINMENT PACKAGES
0181·365·5010

Caught.

Ball watching!

VISITORS

DISABLED

FAMILY

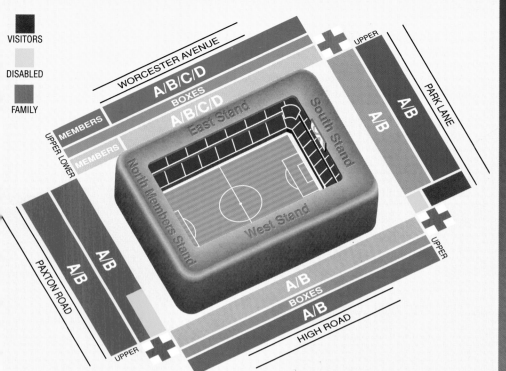

MATCH DAY PRICES

Concession prices in brackets

SOUTH STAND
Capacity 8,461

UPPER

A Premier	£23
B Standard	£20

LOWER

A Premier	£20
B Standard	£17

EAST STAND
Capacity 10,118

UPPER

	Members(A/B)	Non-Members (C/D)
A Premier	£23 (11.50)	
B Standard	£20 (10)	
C Premier		£28
D Standard		£24

LOWER

A Premier	£21 (10.50)	
B Standard	£18 (9)	
C Premier		£23
D Standard		£20

WEST STAND
Capacity 5,837

UPPER

A Premier	£33
B Standard	£28

LOWER

A Premier	£27
B Standard	£22

NORTH MEMBERS
Capacity 6,853

FAMILY

A Premier	£20 (10)
B Standard	£17 (8.50)

FAMILY

A Premier	£18 (9)
B Standard	£15 (7.50)

FOOD AND DRINK

Bar

Tea/Coffee	0.60
Soft Drinks	0.90

Food

Soup	0.60
Hamburger	1.90
Chickenburger	1.90
Veggieburger	1.90
Pie/Pastie	1.50
Hot Dog	1.60
Chips	0.70
Crisps	0.50
Nachos	1.75

MISCELLANEOUS INFORMATION

The following will be screened prior to matches:

Spurs T.V. on Jumbotron screen one hour pre-match programme

PROGRAMME: £1.80

GETTING THERE

White Hart Lane is situated in North London, 6 miles from the centre. Limited parking is available near the ground.

DIRECTIONS

From The North:
From the M1, turn off onto the A1 at Junction 2/3. Join the A406 North Circular Road eastbound and continue for 7 miles. At the Edmonton traffic lights turn right onto the A1010 Fore Street. Continue for 1 mile and White Hart Lane is on the left.

From The North West:
Approaching London on the M40, at Junction 1 stay on the A40 for 10 miles before turning onto the A406 North Circular Road for 13 miles until reaching the Edmonton traffic lights. Then as route for North.

From The West:
Approaching London on the M4, turn off onto the A406 North Circular Road at Junction 1 and continue for 16 miles until reaching the Edmonton traffic lights. Then as route for North.

From The South West:
From the M3 turn off onto the M25 at Junction 2. Continue for 10 miles until you reach Junction 15 at which point turn off onto the M4. Then as route for the West.

From The East:
From the M11 turn off onto the A406 at Junction 4 and continue for 6 miles. At the Edmonton traffic lights turn left onto the A1010 Fore Street. Continue for 1 mile and White Hart Lane is on the left.

Seven Sisters tube station is 1.5 miles away. White Hart Lane Main Line is 3 minutes walk, Northumberland Park, 7 minutes.

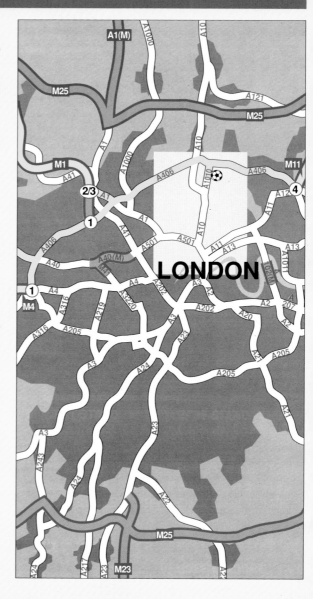

TOTTENHAM HOTSPUR

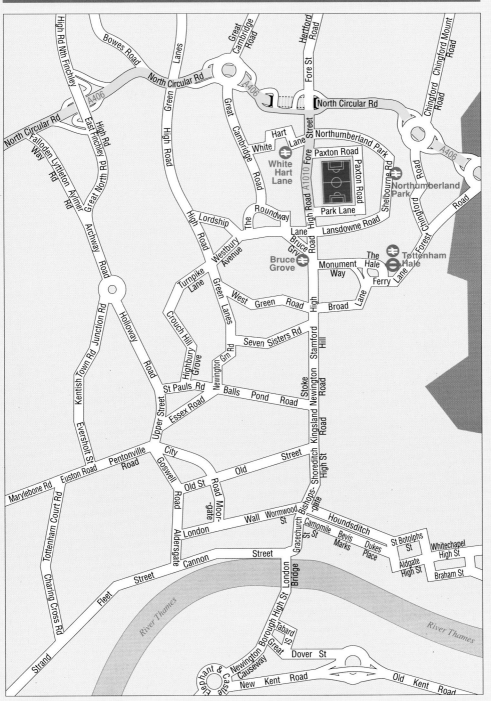

West Ham United FC
Boleyn Ground
Green Street
Upton Park
London E13 9AZ

Club Number: 0181·548·2748
Fax Number: 0181·548·2758
Tickets: 0181·548·2700

INFORMATION HOTLINES

ClubCall: **0891·12 11 65***

*Calls cost 49p per minute peak, 39p per minute off peak

CLUB SHOPS

HAMMERS MERCHANDISE
Boleyn Ground, Green Street, Upton Park
Opening Times:
Monday-Friday: 9.30am-5.00pm
Match Saturdays: 9.30am-5.30pm
Match Sundays: 9.30am-5.30pm
Match Evenings: 9.30am-10.00pm
Tel: 0181·548·2722
Fax: 0181·548·2759
Mail Order Service: 0181·548·2730

BOOKING INFORMATION

General Enquiries: 0181·548·2748
Recorded Information: 0181·472·3322
Credit Cards (Members):   0171·413·9104
Credit Cards (Non-Members): 0171·413·9103
Travel Club: 0181·548·2700

SPECIAL PACKAGES

RESTAURANT
Promotions Department: 0181·548·2777

STADIUM TOURS
Community Department: 0181·548·2707

CORPORATE HOSPITALITY/SPONSORSHIP/ MATCH BALL
Promotions Department
Sue Page: 0181·548·2777

T⊕FFS®

100% NOSTALGIA GUARANTEED

The philosophy behind the formation of TOFFS (The Old Fashioned Football Shirt Company) was, quite simply, to re-create classic cotton football shirts of a high quality (pre-advertising and pre-polyester) all of which would be manufactured in the United Kingdom.

Classic, 100% cotton football shirts from 1885 to 1975 is all we make - and we're good at what we do.

You can't change history three times in a season!

For FREE colour brochure write to:
P.O. Box 71, Gateshead, Tyne & Wear NE11 0UZ
or phone: 0191 491 3500 fax: 0191 491 3305.

THE OLD FASHIONED
FOOTBALL SHIRT COMPANY

"The finest replica shirt makers in the land"...... 90 Minutes

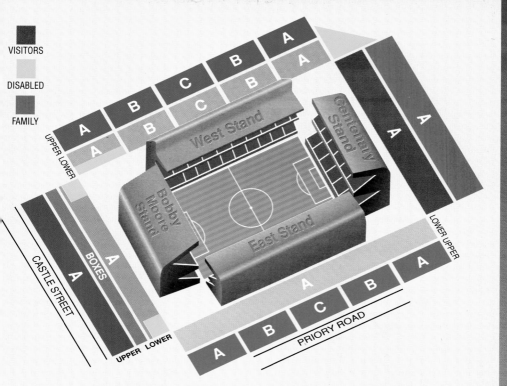

VISITORS

DISABLED

FAMILY

MATCH DAY PRICES

Concession prices in brackets

WEST STAND
Capacity 7,994

UPPER
Block A	£19 (13)
Block B	£23 (13)
Block C	£25 (13)

LOWER
Block A	£19 (13)
Block B	£23 (13)
Block C	£25 (13)

CENTENARY STAND
Capacity 5,646

FAMILY
Block A	£19 (10)

VISITORS
Block A	£18 (10)

EAST STAND
Capacity 4,699

UPPER
Block A	£19 (13)
Block B	£23 (13)
Block C	£25 (13)

LOWER
Block A	£22 (13)

BOBBY MOORE
Capacity 7,558

UPPER
Block A	£21 (13)

LOWER
Block A	£21 (13)

Games against Manchester United, Arsenal, Liverpool, Newcastle, Tottenham and Chelsea are subject to a £4 surcharge on the standard price.

FOOD AND DRINK

Bar
Bitter	TBA
Lager	TBA
Tea/Coffee	TBA
Soft Drinks	TBA

Food
Quarter Pounder With Cheese	TBA
Pies	TBA
Hot Dogs	TBA
Chips	TBA

MISCELLANEOUS INFORMATION

Video Walls in two corners showing pre and post match highlights

Supporters need to get off at Upton Park Tube

PROGRAMME: £2.00

GETTING THERE

Upton Park is in London's East End, approximately 7 miles from London's city centre. There is usually ample parking in the streets around the ground.

DIRECTIONS

From The North:
From the M1, turn off onto the A1 at Junction 2/3. Join the A406 North Circular Road and continue east for 17 miles until the junction with the A214 Barking Road. Turn right into Barking Road and continue for 2 miles, turning right into Green Street. Upton Park is on the right.

From The North West:
Approaching London on the M40, at Junction 1 stay on the A40 for 10 miles before turning onto the A406 North Circular Road eastbound. Stay on this road for 23 miles until the junction with the A214 Barking Road. Then as route for North.

From The West:
Approaching London on the M4, turn off onto the A406 North Circular Road eastbound. Stay on this road for 26 miles until the junction with the A214 Barking Road. Then as route for North.

From The South West:
From the M3 turn off onto the M25 at Junction 2. Continue for 10 miles until you reach Junction 15 at which point turn off onto the M4. Then as route for the West.

From The East:
From the M11 turn off onto the A406 at Junction 4 for 4 miles until the junction with the A214 Barking Road. Then as route for North.

The nearest tube stations are Upton Park and East Ham.

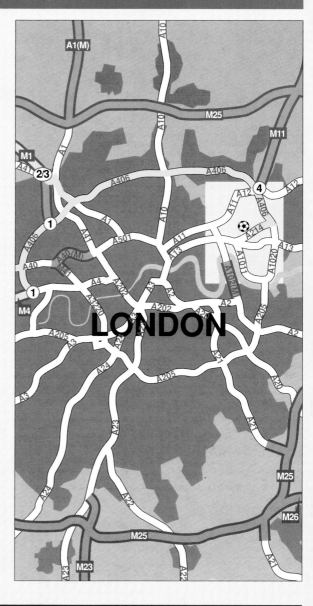

WEST HAM UNITED

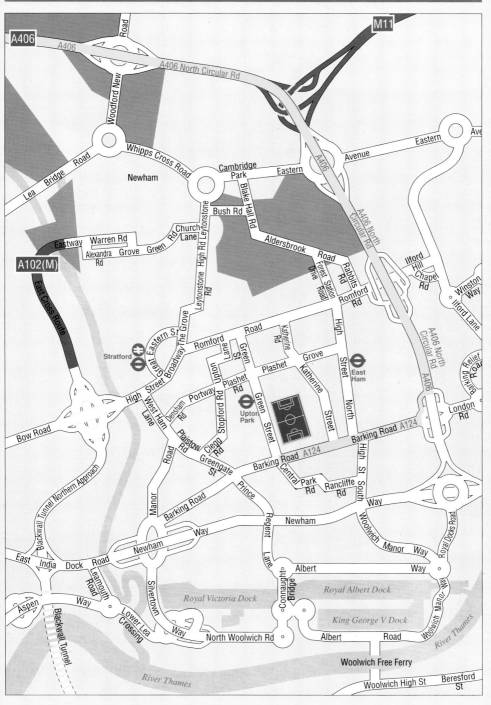

TODAY'S DESKTOP. TOMORROW'S TECHNOLOGY.

The Elonex Low Profile Desktop PC is a deceptively slimline machine. Less than 11cm deep, it already exceeds the internal capacity of many bulkier computers. Better still, it has been built with fast-changing chip technology in mind. It accepts all Intel's Pentium ® Pro processors and will handle tomorrow's even faster and hotter CPUs. Upgrading has never been easier – with simple two-screw access and a standard-size motherboard, the Elonex PC-6200H/I has been designed to let you take maximum advantage of new developments, as they happen.

And while you're waiting for technology to catch up, you'll have some impressive features as standard and a flexible range of configurations to choose from. All in an elegant desktop.

THE ELONEX PC-6200H/I
Ahead of the game.

Machine Specifications

- 200MHz Pentium Pro processor with 256KB L2 cache
- 16MB EDO RAM (expandable to 128MB)
- 2GB IDE hard disk drive
- Dual PCI EIDE Mode 4 controller
- Up to 5 expansion slots (2 x PCI, 3 x ISA)
- Up to 5 drive bays
- 64-bit PCI graphics accelerator (2MB video RAM as standard)
- 15-inch non-interlaced SVGA monitor
- Keyboard and mouse
- Pre-loaded with Windows NT™ Workstation 3.51
- 12 months extendible on-site maintenance
- Access to unlimited technical support (UK mainland only)

London
Tel: 0181-452 4444
Fax: 0181-452 6422

Bradford
Tel: 01274-307226
Fax: 01274-307294

Cumbernauld
Tel: 01236-452052
Fax: 01236-452254

Elonex on the Internet:
http://www.elonex.co.uk

PENTIUM®PRO
PROCESSOR

Wimbledon FC
Selhurst Park Stadium
South Norwood
London SE25 6PY

Club Number: 0181·771·2233
Fax Number: 0181·768·0641
Tickets: 0181·771·8841
Ticket Hotline: 0891·51 61 61*

INFORMATION HOTLINES

ClubCall: **0891·12 11 75***

*Calls cost 49p per minute peak, 39p per minute off peak

CLUB SHOPS

WIMBLEDON FC
Selhurst Park Stadium
Opening Times:
Monday-Friday: 9.30am-5.00pm
Match Saturdays: 10.00am-3.00pm
Match Sundays: 10.00am-4.00pm
Match Evenings: 10.00am-8.00pm
Tel: 0181·768·6100
Fax: 0181·653·4708
Mail Order Tel: 0181·768·6100

BOOKING INFORMATION

General Enquiries: 0181·771·8841
Credit Card Bookings: 0181·771·8841
Travel Club: 0171·771·8841
Recorded Info: 0181·768·6060
Junior Crazy Gang: 0181·771·2233

SPECIAL PACKAGES

RESTAURANT FACILITIES
Sharon Sillitoe: 0181·771·2233

CORPORATE HOSPITALITY/SPONSORSHIP/
MATCH BALL
Sharon Sillitoe: 0181·771·2233

GROUP RATES/SCHOOLS
Steve Rooke: 0181·221·2233

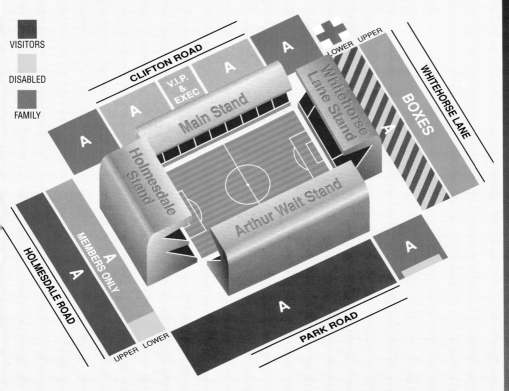

VISITORS

DISABLED

FAMILY

MATCH DAY PRICES

Concession prices in brackets

MAIN STAND
Capacity 6,000

SINGLE TIER	
Block A	£20 (10)

FAMILY	
Block A	£10 (5)

HOLMESDALE ROAD
Capacity 8,000

UPPER	
Block A	£11 (6)

LOWER	
Block A	£11 (6)

WHITEHORSE LANE
Capacity 2,245

LOWER	
Block A	£11 (6)

VISITORS	
Block A	£15

ARTHUR WAIT STAND
Capacity 10,000

VISITORS	
Block A	£15

FAMILY VISITORS	
Block A	£10 (5)

Family areas in the Main Stand and all of the Holmesdale Road Stand are restricted to Crazy Gang Members and bonafide guests. Note that the Whitehorse Lane Stand is used by either home fans or visitors depending on the game.

FOOD AND DRINK

Bar

Beer	1/2 Pint	1.00
	1 Pint	1.95
Spirits		1.50
Fruit Juice		0.80
Mixer		0.75
Tea		0.80
Coffee		1.00

Food

Hot Dog	1.50
Burger	1.50

MISCELLANEOUS INFORMATION

Football in the Community Programmes

Pre-match and half-time DJ playing the latest chart music

PROGRAMME: £1.80

GETTING THERE

Wimbledon play at Selhurst Park in South London, nine miles from the city centre. Parking is allowed in most of the neighbourhood streets and it is usually possible to leave the car quite close to the stadium.

DIRECTIONS

From the North:
Approaching on the M1, exit at Junction 1 onto the A406 North Circular Road. Keep on the North Circular until Chiswick roundabout, then take the A205 South Circular which joins the A3 to Wandsworth. Follow the one-way system and turn right onto the A214 Trinity Road, through Tooting Bec to Streatham. Turn onto the A23 Streatham High Road and left onto the A214 Crown Lane. At the junction turn right onto the A215 Beulah Hill and then right into Whitehorse Lane. The ground is on the left.

From the North West:
Approaching on the M40, continue straight onto the A40 until you meet the A406 North Circular. Then as route for North.

From the West:
Approaching on the M4, exit at Junction 1 Chiswick Roundabout onto the A205 South Circular. Then as route for North.

From the South West:
Approaching on the M3, continue onto the A316 until the junction with the A205 South Circular. Then as route for North.

There are two train stations nearby - Selhurst and Norwood. Both are about five minutes walking distance from Selhurst Park.

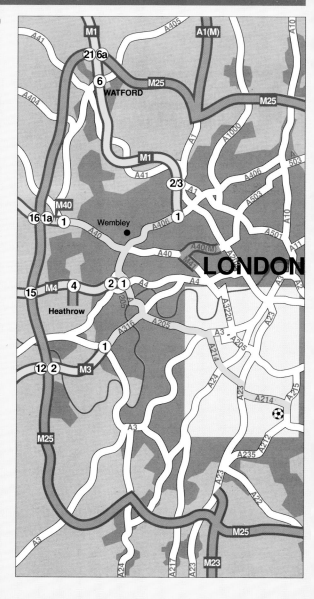

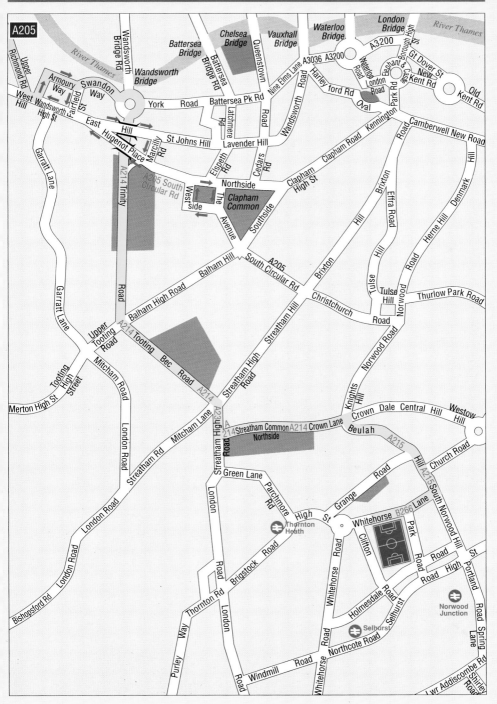

Newcastle ⚽ Sunderland

⚽ Middlesbrough

Blackburn ⚽

⚽ Leeds

Liverpool ⚽ ⚽ Manchester

⚽ Sheffield

Derby ⚽ ⚽ Nottingham

⚽ Leicester

Birmingham ⚽ ⚽ Coventry

London ⚽

Southampton ⚽

	Birmingham	Blackburn	Coventry	Derby	Leeds	Leicester	Liverpool	Manchester	Middlesbrough	Newcastle	Nottingham	Sheffield	Southampton	Sunderland
Sunderland														
Southampton														317
Sheffield													206	130
Nottingham												42	162	156
Newcastle											159	133	320	3
Middlesbrough										38	128	100	288	125
Manchester									104	136	67	40	201	133
Liverpool								33	134	167	103	73	235	164
Leicester							110	95	154	188	28	68	136	185
Leeds						97	73	43	62	96	72	35	230	93
Derby					75	28	87	59	130	165	15	35	157	162
Coventry				43	117	24	113	99	175	209	50	75	114	206
Blackburn			122	86	48	117	40	25	101	118	97	63	239	115
Birmingham		106	19	39	120	43	99	87	174	209	53	79	128	206
London	116	214	107	107	195	101	205	185	245	276	114	165	76	273